ROMANS

A COMMENTARY BY
CARROLL ROBERSON

Published by Innovo Publishing, LLC
www.innovopublishing.com
1-888-546-2111

Publishing quality books, eBooks, audiobooks, music, screenplays & courses for the Christian & wholesome markets since 2008.

ROMANS

ISBN: 978-1-61314-944-7

Cover Design & Interior Layout: Innovo Publishing, LLC

Printed in the United States of America
U.S. Printing History
First Edition: 2023

CONTENTS

INTRODUCTION

With all of the other commentaries that have been written on the book of Romans, what justifies another volume? This author's conviction is that the *Jewish context* has been overlooked. Most of the commentaries on Romans are written with an anti-Semitic perspective, or from a denominational, institutionalized, western-world interpretation, many times in such scholarly fashion that the common man cannot grasp what is being said. One of the goals is to write this commentary on the complex book of Romans with an easy-to-read style. This author will strive to uncover the contextual meanings of the verses in a simplified manner.

The Apostle Paul was writing in Greek because that was the primary language of the people who lived in Rome. He was trained in the Jewish rabbinical schools of Israel, and most of his thoughts were from the Hebrew mind. The book of Romans is not just a New Testament book for *Gentile* Christians, but a continuation of the Hebrew Old Testament, with the Jewish Apostle Paul using Hebrew terms and terminologies in the way he would ask questions and the style in which he gave the answers. Romans cannot be understood without a reference to the Jewish-Roman world in which Paul lived. His Jewish traditions were such a major part of the Apostle's thought process. Through the inspiration of the Holy Spirit, Paul was writing to several small congregations, mostly house churches in and around Rome in the first century. The Christians in Rome became a large community by the year 64AD. The book was written to the Christian *community* in Rome, or *believers living in Rome.* As we study **Romans 16,** there were at least 15 congregations, and Paul mentions more people by name in this book than any other of his epistles. Most of Paul's epistles addressed specific problems the churches were going through, but Romans is different in that he is focusing more on God's great plan of redemption for mankind.

The reason why there were believers in Christ in Rome was not because Paul started a church there, but because many Jews and *strangers from Rome* heard the Apostle Peter preach on the Day of Pentecost in **Acts 2.** After hearing and believing the message that Peter preached about Jesus being Israel's Messiah, they went back to Rome and formed churches without the presence of even *one* of the apostles. This is why Paul wants to write to them with some deep profound truths that they may not have known, and that he had a desire to visit them.

Paul would use pronouns such as *(we, our, us)* to associate himself with the Jewish readers, while using pronouns such as *(you, your)* to refer to the Gentile readers. With the plans that God had announced through His prophets for Israel, where did the *Gentile* believers in Jesus Christ fit in? Paul was deeply concerned that the *Gentiles* did not forget their Jewish roots and realize that they were not the *natural branch, but were grafted into Israel.*

Other than the life and ministry of Jesus the Christ in the four gospels, and the Acts of the early church, Romans has been called the most important book in the New Testament. No other book has played such an important role in forming the major doctrines of Christianity than the book of Romans.

Some of the themes and subjects of Romans are difficult to understand, as Peter would later write:

> ***And account that the longsuffering of our Lord is salvation; even as our beloved brother Paul also according to the wisdom given unto him hath written unto you; As also in all his epistles, speaking in them of these things; in which are some things hard to be understood, which they that are unlearned and unstable wrest, as they do also the other scriptures, unto their own destruction.*** **2 Peter 3:15-16**

Authorship and Date

There is little debate that the author of the book of Romans is the Apostle Paul. He writes from the house of *Gaius* who was saved under Paul's ministry in Corinth, Greece. (**Romans 16:22-23)** Paul wrote in **I Cor. 1:14,** that he had baptized Gaius while in Corinth. The letter to the Romans was taken and delivered to the community by *Phoebe*, a notable woman who lived in Cenchrea, a harbor in Corinth. **(Romans 16:1-2)** The closest date of Paul's writing is the winter of 56-57AD.

CHAPTER ONE

Paul Connects to the Christians in Rome

Romans 1:1-2 - ***Paul, a servant of Jesus Christ, called to be an apostle, separated unto the gospel of God, (Which he had promised afore by his prophets in the holy scriptures,)***

The way that Paul introduces himself was a common way of salutation in Jewish literature of the period. After being a preacher of the gospel for over 20 years, Paul realized more than ever that he was first a *servant of Jesus Christ* and then was *called to be an apostle.* Paul wanted the Roman believers to know that they were reading a letter not from someone writing out of his own invention. Paul had been *separated* as a messenger to bring the *gospel of God* that belongs to the God of heaven. A man named *Saul* had once been set apart to be a Pharisee, but now *Paul* had been set apart for the spreading of the gospel of Jesus the Messiah. The word *"God"* occurs 153 times in the book of Romans, more than any other New Testament book.

The gospel had been *promised afore by the prophets of God in the holy scriptures.* This viewpoint goes back to our

Lord Jesus Himself. **(Luke 24:25-27, 44-47)** The gospel of Israel's Messiah is rooted in the Old Testament: the *Torah,* the *Prophets,* the *Psalms,* and the *Historical Writings.* In the Roman world that Paul lived in, most of the people were interested in some new philosophy, but Paul came with something that was *new* and *old.* The prophets of Israel did not know the time when Israel's Messiah would arrive, but they knew that in the fullness of time He would be revealed. Paul had been given the unique privilege of being called to take this *mystery* to the Gentiles. **(Ephesians 3:1-9)**

> **Romans 1:3-4 -** ***Concerning his Son Jesus Christ our Lord, which was made of the seed of David according to the flesh; And declared to be the Son of God with power, according to the spirit of holiness, by the resurrection from the dead:***

Like the sun is the center of the universe, *the Son Jesus Christ our Lord* is the center of the gospel. The Lord Jesus Christ was a specific Person with a specific identity. He was divine, but He was also human. He was made *the seed of David according to the flesh, and was declared the Son of God with power.* Genealogy was very important during the time Paul was writing, and he wanted the Roman Christians to know that what God promised to David in **2 Samuel 7:12** was fulfilled in this man Jesus Christ. Notice that Paul refers to the Holy Spirit as *the spirit of holiness.* The same Holy Spirit that raised Jesus from the dead is also the same *Spirit of holiness* that produces a life of holiness in the believer. **(Romans 8:11-13)**

The real proof that Jesus is the Son of God is His own *resurrection* that was prefigured in men like *Melchizedek, Enoch, and Elijah*. It was not just one single event in the life of Christ, but a sweeping reality that started something that would forever change the world. What happened in the little nation of Israel had now made its way to Rome and would go into the rest of the world. Everyone who believes in Jesus as the Son of God now has the promise of eternal life and his own resurrection. This rich gold mine of truth is where Paul will draw the doctrines of this epistle. The destiny of every human being is in the hands of Jesus Christ.

> ***And if Christ be not raised, your faith is vain; ye are yet in your sins. Then they also which are fallen asleep in Christ are perished. If in this life only we have hope in Christ, we are of all men most miserable.*** **I Cor. 15:17-19**
>
> ***But now is Christ risen from the dead, and become the firstfruits of them that slept.*** **I Cor. 15:20**
>
> ***I am he that liveth, and was dead; and, behold, I am alive for evermore, Amen; and have the keys of hell and of death.*** **Rev. 1: 18**
>
> **Romans 1:5-6 -** ***By whom we have received grace and apostleship, for obedience to the faith among all nations, for his name: Among whom are ye also the called of Jesus Christ:***

Paul is being modest when he uses the plural pronoun *"we,"* because it is the singular equivalent of *I.* He is stating that his conversion and *apostleship* was given to him all from God's grace. God had given Paul the revelations of the mystery of the gospel in order to produce *obedience to the faith among all nations.* Faith in Christ is a form of obedience, and the result of having true faith will produce a life of obedient living.

> ***Then said they unto him, What shall we do, that we might work the works of God? Jesus answered and said unto them, This is the work of God, that ye believe on him whom he hath sent.*** **John 6:28-29**

The gospel of Jesus Christ was so enormous that it would impact *all nations,* and it would bring glory and honor to the name of *Yeshua Ha Mashiach,* or Jesus the Messiah!

The fact that these Jews and Gentiles in Rome had heard the gospel of Christ and came to believe in Him identified them as *the called of Jesus Christ.*

> **Romans 1:7 -** ***To all that be in Rome, beloved of God, called to be saints: Grace to you and peace from God our Father, and the Lord Jesus Christ.***

The church in Rome was not started or organized by the Apostle Paul. However, the believers are still considered to be *the beloved of God and called to be saints.* Paul could not and did not save anyone; it was the workings of the Holy Spirit that drew them to salvation. The term *beloved* is synonymous with *chosen, called, elected, and saints.* Paul considered them to be his brethren in Christ even though he had never seen them.

Here Paul inserts a Jewish greeting that was the custom of his day. Paul's desire was that the believers in Rome would continue to experience God's abundant *grace and peace,* which came from *God the Father and the Lord Jesus Christ.* God had brought *peace* between man and God through Jesus His Son, as well as *peace* between Jews and Gentiles.

> **Romans 1:8-10 - *First, I thank my God through Jesus Christ for you all, that your faith is spoken of throughout the whole world. For God is my witness, whom I serve with my spirit in the gospel of his Son, that without ceasing I make mention of you always in my prayers; Making request, if by any means now at length I might have a prosperous journey by the will of God to come unto you.***

The faith of the Christians in Rome had such a good reputation, that people were talking about them throughout the known world. Wow! They were geographically located in the Aegean Sea, the middle of the Roman Empire, where the news had spread across land and sea about their faith in Christ. While Rome was known for the unbelievable sins of incest, paganism, and idolatry, just to name a few, these believers were strong in their faith in Christ. God was protecting them from the evil that surrounded them. Their persecution would eventually lead to the martyrdom of Paul, but their rewards would have an abundant entrance into God's kingdom.

Paul wanted them to know that he was not just saying words like *"I am praying for you"* without actually praying for them. *God was his witness* that he prayed for them *without ceasing.* This is one reason why their faith was strong and why their church community was growing. Paul also prayed that he would be blessed to be able *to come to them* on his way to Spain, but he knew it would depend on *the will of God.* Paul had learned his lesson through many experiences that the hand of the Lord determined where he went. In Jewish thought, praying for others was considered *a worship of the heart.* What a different world we would see if all believers in Christ would love each other and sincerely pray for one another!

> **Romans 1:11-12 -** ***For I long to see you, that I may impart unto you some spiritual gift, to the end ye may be established; That is, that I may be comforted together with you by the mutual faith both of you and me.***

Paul wanted to see the Roman believers in person so that he could *give* to them and *receive* as well. He wanted their faith to be more established in their hearts so they could face the trials and persecutions that would come to them later. As great of a Christian as Paul was, he needed encouragement in his own life. The calling of God on his life was real and he knew that he would never turn back, but he still needed the fellowship of other believers. There is no one who is so strong in the faith that he does not need other believers to encourage him from time to time.

> **Romans 1:13 -** ***Now I would not have you ignorant, brethren, that oftentimes I purposed to come unto you, (but was let hitherto,) that I might have some fruit among you also, even as among other Gentiles.***

Paul wanted the Christians in Rome not to be uninformed or ignorant to the fact that he desired to see them not only one time. He had *purposed* oftentimes to come to them. Just as Jesus desired to see spiritual fruit among His brethren when He walked in Jerusalem, **(Luke 13:6-9)** Paul had such compassion on the Roman believers that he wanted to see them flourish spiritually and be filled with joy. Paul felt the responsibility not only to share the gospel of Christ with the unbelievers in the *Gentile world,* but he wanted to see them become disciples and grow in their faith. We find this same thought when Paul wrote to the first church in Europe, the Philippian church:

> ***Nevertheless to abide in the flesh is more needful for you. And having this confidence, I know that I shall abide and continue with you all for your furtherance and joy of faith; That your rejoicing may be more abundant in Jesus Christ for me by my coming to you again. Only let your conversation be as it becometh the gospel of Christ: that whether I come and see you, or else be absent, I may hear of your affairs, that ye stand fast in one spirit, with one mind striving together for the faith of the gospel;*** **(Phil. 1:24-27)**

> **Romans 1:14-15 -** ***I am debtor both to the Greeks, and to the Barbarians; both to the wise, and to the unwise. So, as much as in me is, I am ready to preach the gospel to you that are at Rome also.***

Why would Paul feel as though he was indebted to the Gentile world? It is not that the Gentiles had some claim on the Apostle Paul, but that the Lord Jesus Christ had a claim on him! Paul felt that he was a *debtor* not only to those within the Greek culture of the Roman Empire, but also to the *Barbarians* who were outside of the Greek culture. While both the Greeks who lived in Rome and the *Barbarians* were considered to be pagans by the Jews, the Greeks were refined and cultured, while the *Barbarians* were not. Being able to minister the gospel in the capital city of the Roman Empire was a necessary capstone in his Gentile apostleship, so Paul says *I am ready to preach the gospel to you that are at Rome also.*

Unlike Alexander, the Caesars, or Napoleon, Paul would go into Rome without the protection of a huge military army. Paul would march with Christ alone!

> **Romans 1:16-17 - *For I am not ashamed of the gospel of Christ: for it is the power of God unto salvation to every one that believeth; to the Jew first, and also to the Greek. For therein is the righteousness of God revealed from faith to faith: as it is written, The just shall live by faith.***

This author believes that this passage is not only the major theme of the book of Romans, but it has been misrepresented in many cases. Paul is not *ashamed,* (the Greek *epaisxýnomai*) not *disgraced,* not *embarrassed,* not *afraid,* not *worried about being singled out,* to take the gospel into Rome, a major city of great philosophers, mythological gods and goddesses, sexual perversion, and idolatry. Paul knew *the gospel of Christ* had the *power to save, rescue,* and *to deliver* the Hellenized Jews and pagan Gentiles from their sins. We need to remember that the *power* is not in us, but the *power* is in the gospel of Christ! That is why we must stay true in preaching the gospel to the lost. The message of Christ is accompanied by the *power* of the Holy

Spirit, who knows every person and what it will take to deliver them from the wrath to come. Hallelujah! Paul had been given his apostleship from God with the commission to go to the Jews first. Why? God would use the Jews to help bring Jesus the Jewish Messiah into the world, and in doing so would be a *light to the Gentiles.* **(Isaiah 42:6, 49:6, Luke 2:32)** The believing Gentiles would become part of the commonwealth of Israel. **(Ephesians 2:12-13)**

"For therein is the righteousness of God revealed from faith to faith: as it is written, The just shall live by faith." The gospel of Christ is a message that reveals the *righteousness of God!* For God to deliver sinful man, it must be manifested consistent with God's righteous character. Paul is thinking in terms of the righteousness of God being imputed to believers because of his words: *from faith to faith.* The KJV translation is hard to understand and a good rendering would be *by faith for faith*. The *righteousness of God* is attained by means of faith and is bestowed upon those who have faith in Christ. This shows how important it is for us to have faith in the finished work of Christ. This author believes that this is one of the most important subjects, not only in the book of Romans, but throughout the entire Bible. Sinful man cannot enter into eternal life and go to a perfect heaven without God's righteousness being granted. God's righteousness is not revealed to *condemn* the sinner, but it is *given* to the sinner who has faith in Jesus as the Son of God, apart from the works of the law, and apart from any good deeds. It has nothing to do with good works, period! It is available through the work that Christ did. This is the victory that a Christian experiences knowing that he has God's righteousness! Hallelujah! Paul looks at this thought more in **Romans 4.**

Paul did not invent this theology, and as he would begin his ministry in each city within the Jewish synagogues, he wanted them to know that this was a principle that was taught over 700 years before Christ as written by the prophet **Habakkuk** in chapter **2** verse **4**: *"but the just shall live by his faith."* This is also a direct reference to the Messiah of Israel as being the *Righteous Branch of David:*

> ***In those days, and at that time, will I cause the Branch of righteousness to grow up unto David; and he shall execute judgment and righteousness in the land.*** **Jeremiah 33:15**
>
> ***In his days Judah shall be saved, and Israel shall dwell safely: and this is his name whereby he shall be called, The Lord Our Righteousness.*** **Jeremiah 23:6**

One of God's Hebrew names is *Yehovah Tzidkenu,* the Lord our Righteousness!

THE GUILT OF THE HUMAN RACE

> **Romans 1:18 -** ***For the wrath of God is revealed from heaven against all ungodliness and unrighteousness of men, who hold the truth in unrighteousness;***

The greatest peril of the human race is to face *the wrath of God.* This wrath is *revealed* from God's perfect heaven to a deserving human race. Paul is demonstrating that God's righteousness is necessary to deliver people from *God's wrath.* It is not just that God is angry with man, but His wrath is a result of His perfect righteousness. Unless an individual embraces the cross of Christ and the blood that he shed on the cross to cover his sins, he is under the wrath of God. Jesus talked about *the wrath of God:*

> ***He that believeth on the Son hath everlasting life: and he that believeth not the Son shall not see life; but the wrath of God abideth on him.*** **John 3:36**

"against all ungodliness and unrighteousness of men, who hold the truth in unrighteousness;" - *Ungodliness* is referring to man's perverse behavior with one another. This will be spelled out more specifically in the following verses. The *unrighteousness of men* is how man sins against God and even suppresses God's truth in his own conscience. Sinful man fights against, disregards, and deliberately goes against God's truth. There are many ways in which this is done, and Paul may be referring to the serious idolatry in the Roman culture at that time. They were ignoring God's moral laws and rebelled against their Creator. Someone who does not have the Spirit of Christ living inside of him only has the flesh and the natural mind to serve his evil inclinations.

> **Romans 1:19-20** - ***Because that which may be known of God is manifest in them; for God hath shewed it unto them. For the invisible things of him from the creation of the world are clearly seen, being understood by the things that are made, even his eternal power and Godhead; so that they are without excuse:***

Sinful man cannot charge God with hiding Himself from them. There is a clear witness of God in the visible world, and it has been *manifested to them.* The fact that sinful man would even consider that the universe was designed and created without the Almighty God is absurd and ludicrous. Even someone who has never heard the gospel of Jesus Christ can see the works of the invisible God in creation. God's righteousness and *eternal power* have been revealed in the glory and beauty of His creation. This passage in the *Psalms* comes to mind:

> ***The heavens declare the glory of God; and the firmament sheweth his handywork. Day unto day uttereth speech, and night unto night sheweth knowledge. There is no speech nor language, where their voice is not heard.*** **Psalm 19:1-3**

"so that they are without excuse:" - Again, Paul may have been telling the Roman believers that when they see others in that first-century culture worshipping idols and gods of stone, they could not diminish God's eternal power. Man is accountable to God and still abides in darkness if he does not see God's attributes through creation.

Sinful man is *without excuse* in knowing that God does exist. The question may arise, *"Can someone be saved by just looking at creation?"* This author thinks no! If that were the case, then people from other faiths and religions could be saved in another way other than coming through the Lord Jesus Christ. Jesus made it very clear in **John 14:6:**

> ***Jesus saith unto him, I am the way, the truth, and the life: <u>no man cometh unto the Father, but by me.</u>***

Romans 1:21-22 - *Because that, when they knew God, they glorified him not as God, neither were thankful; but became vain in their imaginations, and their foolish heart was darkened. Professing themselves to be wise, they became fools,*

It was not that man did not know that God existed. He refused to glorify God and created forms and ideas more comfortable to his corrupt mind and worshiped a self-made image of God. Knowledge of God is totally different than having a relationship with God through Jesus the Son of God. Someone can know his theology and be a scholar in his doctrine, but if he is not *thankful* enough to accept Christ and what He did for him on the cross, he is a lost individual. Let us review the historical process of how man has deteriorated:

- ***Did not glorify God as God***
- ***Man was not thankful for even the gift of life***
- ***Man engaged in his own imaginations***
- ***The result was a foolish heart that was darkened***

"Professing themselves to be wise, they became fools," - Man is so sinful that he is even self-confident about his own ignorance. We can see this even in our own day with all of the intellectual studies in astronomy and physics that this universe had to have a Divine Creator. Still man refuses to believe, and he thinks *he is wise but in reality he is a fool.* Being *wise* in one's own eyes leads to serving one's *foolish* inclinations. When man rejects God and what Christ did on the cross, he will fall for anything. Because man's heart is darkened, God imparts judgment and allows the unbelievers to suffer His wrath. It is so sad to look at our world today and to think how many people who were created in the image of God are good for nothing and will perish in the end. There are numerous verses in the Old Testament that talk about sinful man's foolish heart:

> ***The fool hath said in his heart, There is no God. They are corrupt, they have done abominable works, there is none that doeth good.*** **Psalm 14:1**
>
> ***This evil people, which refuse to hear my words, which walk in the imagination of their heart, and walk after other gods, to serve them, and to worship them, shall even be as this girdle, which is good for nothing.*** **Jeremiah 13:10**
>
> **Romans 1:23 -** ***And changed the glory of the uncorruptible God into an image made like to corruptible man, and to birds, and fourfooted beasts, and creeping things.***

The glory of God was manifested to Israel of old, and they turned His glory into the image of animals as in **Psalm 106:20.** This had evolved over the centuries into Paul's day when man had changed the glory of God into idols in the image of *mortal man, birds, four-footed creatures, and even reptiles.* Again, when man refuses to see upward and all around him the Eternal God in creation, he turns downward and will even worship his own gods made out of silver, gold, wood, and stone. The Roman world in which the believers in Rome resided had a polytheistic Pantheon dedicated to all of the 12 major gods and goddesses:

- **Jupiter** was the master of the gods and the main god of the Romans.
- **Juno** was the wife of Jupiter, the goddess of women and fertility. Her symbols were a pomegranate and a peacock.
- **Mars** was the god of war, the strongest and most fearsome god, except for Jupiter.
- **Venus** was the goddess of love and beauty.
- **Minerva** was the goddess of wisdom, learning, art crafts and industry. Her symbol was the owl.
- **Neptune** was the powerful god of the sea. His symbol was the trident.
- **Ceres** was the goddess of the harvest, always depicted carrying a bundle of grain.
- **Vulcan** was the blacksmith of the gods and the god of the underworld. If he stroked the furnace too hard, volcanoes might erupt. He was the god of blacksmiths and volcanoes.
- **Diana** was the goddess of hunting and a goddess of the moon.
- **Bacchus** was the god of wine and partying. Naturally, he was one of Rome's most popular gods.
- **Mercury** was the messenger of the gods. The wings on his helmet and sandals allowed him to travel very quickly to wherever a god might send him. He was the god of travelers and tradesmen.
- **Vesta** was the goddess of the hearth and home. She was very important to Romans. In her temple a flame

> was always kept burning as the "hearth of Rome." The flame should never go out.

While this may seem farfetched and far removed from our modern-day way of living, the United States is fast becoming a secular nation where children have to study false religions in our public schools and cannot even pray or wear **John 3:16** tee shirts. Almost half of the preachers in the pulpit do not see the world through a biblical worldview anymore. The gods of materialism, wealth, pleasure, sex, and even what America calls *"church"* have taken professing Christians away from the Lord God. In many parts of our nation, little Christian children cannot sing Christmas Carols to celebrate the birth of Jesus, while other children can pray Islamic prayers out loud. Idols stand in most every large city in America today. Is there a servant of Christ in our land? America has turned its back on the God who founded this nation, and judgment is coming!

The Result of Man's Rebellion

> **Romans 1:24-25 - *Wherefore God also gave them up to uncleanness through the lusts of their own hearts, to dishonour their own bodies between themselves: Who changed the truth of God into a lie, and worshipped and served the creature more than the Creator, who is blessed for ever. Amen.***

Paul is not using some new idea by saying that because of man's idolatry and rebellion against God that *He gives them up.* He uses it three times within the next few verses. The English translation is somewhat obscure, but going back to the Old

Testament we can find the true meaning of *God giving up on people.* Here are a few examples:

> ***So I gave them up unto their own hearts' lust: and they walked in their own counsels.*** **Psalm 81:12**

The Hebrew word in this verse for *gave them up* is *shalach*, and it means *"sending."* God *sends away* those who do not retain the truth and dishonored the Creator. God simply hands them over to their own stubbornness and hides His face from them so they are left to walk in their own sinful *counsels.*

> ***And he sent forth*** *"shalach"* ***a raven, which went forth to and fro, until the waters were dried up from off the earth.*** **Genesis 8:7**
>
> ***For we will destroy this place, because the cry of them is waxen great before the face of the LORD: and the LORD hath sent*** *"shalach"* ***us to destroy it.*** **Genesis 19:13**

It is not God's mercy many times that allows people to continue in their evil ways, but it is His wrath that allows them to go on and destroy themselves. Since the majority of the people of Rome and Corinth, the city where Paul was writing from, had dishonored God by misrepresenting Him with creature-like beings, they are given over to satisfy their corrupt desires of the flesh. Without God in their lives, they go so far as to *dishonor their own bodies between themselves.* Sinful man has *changed the truth of God into a lie* and turned the worship of the Creator into *creature worship.* When God is not worshiped as the Creator, immorality is the result. Not only was immorality going on everywhere, it had also turned into idolatrous worship.

This portion of scripture is so dreadful that many preachers down through the centuries thought it was unfit to read in public. People do not like to study about Satan's snares, and therefore this leads to falling into them. There are three nets that Satan used to destroy Israel of old:

* ***The net of lust***
* ***The net of riches***
* ***The net of defiling the worship of God***

> **Romans 1:26-27** - ***For this cause God gave them up unto vile affections: for even their women did change the natural use into that which is against nature: And likewise also the men, leaving the natural use of the woman, burned in their lust one toward another; men with men working that which is unseemly, and receiving in themselves that recompence of their error which was meet.***

The sexual sins that Paul is describing here is homosexuality for the men and lesbianism for the women. This type of sexuality goes against God's design for procreation:

> ***So God created man in his own image, in the image of God created he him; male and female created he them. And God blessed them, and God said unto them, Be fruitful, and multiply, and replenish the earth, and subdue it:*** **Genesis 1:27-28a**

Homosexuality is condemned in both the Old and New Testaments.

> ***Thou shalt not lie with mankind, as with womankind: it is* abomination. Leviticus 18:22**
>
> ***If a man also lie with mankind, as he lieth with a woman, both of them have committed an abomination:*** *(the Hebrew toebah, meaning detestable, loathsome)* ***they shall surely be put to death; their blood shall be upon them.*** **Leviticus 20:13**

Paul lived in a culture where homosexuality was accepted as a part of life for both men and women. Many of the Roman Emperors openly practiced homosexuality often with young boys. Rome even gave a special tax break for homosexual prostitution and gave boy prostitutes a legal holiday. Legal marriage between two men or two women was recognized. Even in Roman times there was a connection between sexual promiscuity and certain diseases. This was part of the *receiving in themselves the recompense of their error.*

At the time of writing this book, the United States has over 70 percent of the population that agree with same-sex marriage. Our public schools are even teaching the little children to just call them *"parents"* instead of *"Mom & Dad."* What was going on in ancient Rome is happening today in our own nation. This is a major sign of the end-times according to what Jesus said:

> ***And as it was in the days of Noe, so shall it be also in the days of the Son of man. They did eat, they drank,***

> ***they married wives, they were given in marriage, until the day that Noe entered into the ark, and the flood came, and destroyed them all. Likewise also as it was in the days of Lot; they did eat, they drank, they bought, they sold, they planted, they builded; But the same day that Lot went out of Sodom it rained fire and brimstone from heaven, and destroyed them all.* Luke 17:26-29**

The question may arise, *"Can anyone be born a homosexual?"* In some cases, Satan is working through procreation as he did in **Genesis 6:4:**

> ***There were giants in the earth in those days; and also after that, when the sons of God came in unto the daughters of men, and they bare children to them, the same became mighty men which were of old, men of renown.***

In Genesis Satan used *sons of God,* the Hebrew *"bene ha elohim,"* or fallen angels to have intercourse with women to create giants, the Hebrew *"nephilim,"* who were a demonic race of people that eventually led to the flood. We are seeing the repeat of this demonic activity in our world today, and it will increase the closer we get to the Second Coming of the Lord Jesus Christ.

The increase in homosexuality in our world today is partially a result of Satan using demon-possessed people to procreate. The majority of homosexuality in men and lesbianism in women is the rebellion and dishonoring of God by his/her own selfish choices. Even Tel-Aviv, the largest city in Israel, is one of the major centers for homosexuality in the

Middle East. Israel, the land of the Bible, is under the judgment of God for this sexual perversion.

> **Romans 1:28 -** ***And even as they did not like to retain God in their knowledge, God gave them over to a reprobate mind, to do those things which are not convenient;***

The third time that God turns the rebellious, perverse people over, he gives them a *reprobate, or debased mind.* This means that they call *evil good* and call *good evil* and have no hope of salvation. In the Old Testament the sin of homosexuality was called *abomination,* and in the New Testament they are turned over to *reprobation.* Could it be this is why our world is disintegrating before our very eyes? This author is reminded of what Paul Harvey said in a 1967 commentary, *"If I Were the Devil"*

> *"If I were the devil … If I were the Prince of Darkness, I'd want to engulf the whole world in darkness. And I'd have a third of its real estate, and four-fifths of its population, but I wouldn't be happy until I had seized the ripest apple on the tree — Thee. So I'd set about however necessary to take over the United States. I'd subvert the churches first — I'd begin with a campaign of whispers. With the wisdom of a serpent, I would whisper to you as I whispered to Eve: 'Do as you please.'*
>
> *To the young, I would whisper that 'The Bible is a myth.' I would convince them that man created God instead of the other way around. I would confide that what's bad is good, and what's good is 'square.' And the old, I would teach to pray, after me, 'Our Father, which art in Washington…*

And then I'd get organized. I'd educate authors in how to make lurid literature exciting, so that anything else would appear dull and uninteresting. I'd threaten TV with dirtier movies and vice versa. I'd pedal narcotics to whom I could. I'd sell alcohol to ladies and gentlemen of distinction. I'd tranquilize the rest with pills.

If I were the devil I'd soon have families at war with themselves, churches at war with themselves, and nations at war with themselves; until each in its turn was consumed. And with promises of higher ratings I'd have mesmerizing media fanning the flames. If I were the devil I would encourage schools to refine young intellects, but neglect to discipline emotions — just let those run wild, until before you knew it, you'd have to have drug sniffing dogs and metal detectors at every schoolhouse door.

Within a decade I'd have prisons overflowing, I'd have judges promoting pornography — soon I could evict God from the courthouse, then from the schoolhouse, and then from the houses of Congress. And in His own churches I would substitute psychology for religion, and deify science. I would lure priests and pastors into misusing boys and girls, and church money. If I were the devil I'd make the symbols of Easter an egg and the symbol of Christmas a bottle.

If I were the devil I'd take from those who have, and give to those who want until I had killed the incentive of the ambitious.

And what do you bet I could get whole states to promote gambling as the way to get rich? I would caution against extremes and hard work in Patriotism, in moral conduct. I would convince the young that marriage is old-fashioned, that swinging is more fun, that what you see on the TV is the way to be. And thus, I could undress you in public, and I could lure you into bed with diseases for which there is no cure. In other words, if I were the devil I'd just keep right on doing what he's doing."

Paul Harvey, good day.

Romans 1:29-31 - *Being filled with all unrighteousness, fornication, wickedness, covetousness, maliciousness; full of envy, murder, debate, deceit, malignity; whisperers, Backbiters, haters of God, despiteful, proud, boasters, inventors of evil things, disobedient to parents, Without understanding, covenantbreakers, without natural affection, implacable, unmerciful:*

Paul then gives a list of the particular manifestations of a reprobate mind. Notice how social acceptable sins like *envy and covetousness* are included right along with the socially unacceptable sins such as *murder.* This list is filled with sins between man and God and between man and man. The list is self-explanatory, but look at the word *implacable.* It is the Greek *"aspondos"* which means *"impossible to change, refuses to make a truce."* When someone has been turned over by God and sent away with a reprobate mind, he does not have the ability to change his evil mind. For example, if you have a disagreement with someone and you go to him trying to make peace, he not only will refuse, he no longer has enough goodness within himself to make peace.

> **Romans 1:32 - *Who knowing the judgment of God, that they which commit such things are worthy of death, not only do the same, but have pleasure in them that do them.***

The grim finale is that the people who have been sent away with a reprobate mind are *worthy of death.* They are worthy of targets of God's wrath. Not only do the people commit such sins, they take pleasure in doing them and actually commend others for doing them. The level of sin is to the level of having respect among other sinners and to make evil a virtue. A good example is the elevation of *gay* sin to the level of an *approvable lifestyle.* The sins of this type of a person cry out for *the judgment of God.*

CHAPTER TWO

THE GUILT OF THE JEW AND THE GENTILE

> **Romans 2:1-3 -** ***Therefore thou art inexcusable, O man, whosoever thou art that judgest: for wherein thou judgest another, thou condemnest thyself; for thou that judgest doest the same things. But we are sure that the judgment of God is according to truth against them which commit such things. And thinkest thou this, O man, that judgest them which do such things, and doest the same, that thou shalt escape the judgment of God?***

Paul continues the argument from the previous chapter that no man has an excuse before God for his behavior. Anyone who *judges* another person has no defense. The would-be *judge* does the same things. Even if someone has been sheltered from a life of the immoral sins that Paul listed in **Romans 1:29-31,** the *sins of the spirit* would still condemn him. All of humanity has the inclination to sin; it is just that sin manifests itself in different ways in each person. The principle that Paul is referring to here was first given by Christ:

> ***He that is without sin among you, let him first cast a stone at her.*** **John 8:7**

A religious Jew who has the Torah cannot point a finger at the Gentiles who do not have the Torah. Just because Israel was the *elect of God, it* does not give them an automatic redemption. The moral Jew cannot *judge* the immoral Gentile while being guilty of the same sins. Just because the Jew did not bow down to idols of stone, he still committed *spiritual idolatry.* The Jews claimed to worship the God of Israel in the Temple in Jerusalem, but the nation rejected Jesus as their Messiah while He walked in their streets. Another example: they would adorn the tombs of the prophets that their forefathers had unjustly killed. Take note of what Jesus said about the religious leaders of His day:

> ***Woe unto you! for ye build the sepulchres of the prophets, and your fathers killed them. Truly ye bear witness that ye allow the deeds of your fathers: for they indeed killed them, and ye build their sepulchres.*** **Luke 11:47-48**

What about those people who are moralists and think they are better than others? Our world is filled with so-called *good* people, but they are also *without excuse.* Sinful man is guilty of comparing himself with other sinful people and not comparing himself to a holy and righteous God. How many times have we known that something was wrong and we did it anyway, taking for granted that God would just forgive us? Sin is a universal problem! There is not anyone who can congratulate himself because he is not like other people. Just being a good moral person does not give anyone a way of escaping God's wrath. The road to hell is filled with good moral people! Deeply buried within the conscience of a moral person is the awareness of God's standards. Like the world of Rome, our world today has lost the reality of God's absolute *truth* in the universe. Today multitudes think their personal theology or their church's belief system are relative.

> **Romans 2:4-5 -** ***Or despisest thou the riches of his goodness and forbearance and longsuffering; not knowing that the goodness of God leadeth thee to repentance? But after thy hardness and impenitent heart treasurest up unto thyself wrath against the day of wrath and revelation of the righteous judgment of God;***

A holy God has shown His *goodness* to us in regard to our *past sins*. He has not judged us yet even though we deserve it, and He has placed our judgment upon Christ on the cross. God's *forbearance* may be considered God's kindness and patience to us regarding our *present sins*. We have all fallen short of His glory, and yet He holds back His *righteous judgment*. God's *longsuffering* may be considered His mercy to us in regard to our *future sins*. He knows that we will sin tomorrow and the next day, yet He holds back His judgment against us all because we belong to Jesus. He is using our mistakes to lead us and to teach us the path of righteousness.

All of these are called *riches* and should lead the guilty Jew and Gentile to *repentance*. God's love for sinful humanity has shown us such *goodness* that we have ignored Him. God's *goodness* should provoke sinful man to turn and start walking with Jesus Christ. God does not *drive* us to repentance, but He *leads* us to repentance. The way that God showed His *goodness* to David and showed him mercy even during his selfish mistakes in the Old Testament inspired these words:

> ***Surely goodness and mercy shall follow me all the days of my life: and I will dwell in the house of the Lord for ever.*** **Psalm 23:6**

When a moral person is judging someone else, he is actually *treasuring up the wrath of God upon himself.* When Jesus came the first time, He showed how much God so loved the world by dying on a tree for *all* sin. In the original transcript the meaning implies that when Jesus returns the second time, the good moral people who have not been regenerated by the Holy Spirit will experience *the wrathfully manifested revelation of the righteous judgment of God* the same as the immoral people. The fundamental truth that Paul is expressing is that all men, moral and immoral, are subject to God's wrath. This is not just something in the future but a present reality. *Asaph,* the chief musician in the Temple, wrote these words centuries before Paul was born:

> ***But unto the wicked God saith, What hast thou to do to declare my statutes, or that thou shouldest take my covenant in thy mouth? Seeing thou hatest instruction, and casteth my words behind thee. When thou sawest a thief, then thou consentedst with him, and hast been partaker with adulterers. Thou givest thy mouth to evil, and thy tongue frameth deceit. Thou sittest and speakest against thy brother; thou slanderest thine own mother's son. These things hast***

thou done, and I kept silence; thou thoughtest that I was altogether such an one as thyself: but I will reprove thee, and set them in order before thine eyes. Now consider this, ye that forget God, lest I tear you in pieces, and there be none to deliver. Whoso offereth praise glorifieth me: and to him that ordereth his conversation aright will I shew the salvation of God. **Psalm 50:16-23**

God's Judgment is Impartial

Romans 2:6-7 - ***Who will render to every man according to his deeds: To them who by patient continuance in well doing seek for glory and honour and immortality, eternal life:***

There are those who take these verses and try to prove that man can be saved by his works, but they read these verses without reading the entire *scope* of what the Jewish Paul is saying and without reading other verses in the New Testament. Of course no one can be saved by good *deeds* as Paul will later make clear in **Romans 3:2, 10, 12, 16** and **Galatians 2:16, 3:2, 10.** Because *biblical faith* produces a life of good *deeds* sometimes, the Bible refers to people who have *faith in Christ* as people with a life of good works or *deeds.* Notice these verses:

For the Son of man shall come in the glory of his Father with his angels; and then he shall reward every man according to his works. **Matthew 16:27**

> ***For we must all appear before the judgment seat of Christ; that every one may receive the things done in his body, according to that he hath done, whether it be good or bad.*** **2 Corinthians 5:10**

> ***And I heard a voice from heaven saying unto me, Write, Blessed are the dead which die in the Lord from henceforth: Yea, saith the Spirit, that they may rest from their labours; and their works do follow them.*** **Revelation 14:13**

> ***And I saw the dead, small and great, stand before God; and the books were opened: and another book was opened, which is the book of life: and the dead were judged out of those things which were written in the books, according to their works.*** **Revelation 20:12**

For the first time Paul refers to eternal realities by the use of the phrase *eternal life.* God will determine every lost individual's *eternal destiny,* and those who receive Christ will receive *eternal life.* God knows how to righteously judge everyone, and the only way that a person can obtain *eternal life* is through faith in the finished work of Christ alone, and who *patiently continues to seek for glory, honor, immortality, and eternal life.*

> **Romans 2:8-10** - ***But unto them that are contentious, and do not obey the truth, but obey unrighteousness, indignation and wrath, Tribulation and anguish, upon every soul of man that doeth evil, of the Jew first, and also of the Gentile; But glory, honour, and peace, to every man that worketh good, to the Jew first, and also to the Gentile:***

Paul is challenging the Christian Jews and Gentiles in Rome to realize and to look at all of the people from God's perspective. God's wrath will be poured out upon *every soul of man that doeth evil.* While no one can be saved without trusting in Jesus Christ, there will be degrees of punishment for the *unbelievers* based on how much light has been given:

> ***But and if that servant say in his heart, My lord delayeth his coming; and shall begin to beat the menservants and maidens, and to eat and drink, and to be drunken; The lord of that servant will come in a day when he looketh not for him, and at an hour when he is not aware, and will cut him in sunder, and will appoint him his portion with the unbelievers. And that servant, which knew his lord's will, and prepared not himself, neither did according to his will, shall be beaten with <u>many stripes</u>. But he that knew not, and did commit things worthy of stripes, shall be beaten with <u>few stripes</u>. For unto whomsoever much is given, of him shall be much required: and to whom men have committed much, of him they will ask the more.*** **Luke 12:45–48**

> ***And the sea gave up the dead which were in it; and death and hell delivered up the dead which were in them: and they were judged every man according to their works.*** **Revelation 20:13**

The Roman world and the world in which we live today would be different if people *could* live a righteous life. Because of man's selfishness, the world is filled with *contention, disobedience, unrighteousness, indignation, wrath, tribulation, anguish, and evil.* The Jews will share in the judgment that is waiting. They will not be excluded just because they are natural born Jews.

"But glory, honour, and peace, to every man that worketh good, to the Jew first, and also to the Gentile:" **-** The Jews and Gentiles will suffer the wrath of God if they *obey unrighteousness,* but they both will receive *glory, honor, and peace if they worketh good.* It needs to be repeated so we will not be confused. The Bible is clear that salvation is by grace alone through faith in the sacrificial death and glorious resurrection of the Son of God. Good works that will count begin at the point of receiving Christ. The Holy Spirit starts to do God's work through our lives once we have been born again.

> ***For it is God which worketh in you both to will and to do of his good pleasure.*** **Philippians 2:13**

> **Romans 2:11 -** ***For there is no respect of persons with God.***

Some of the Jewish rabbis taught that God showed partiality to the Jews, and that He will judge the Gentiles more harshly because they were called *benei berit,* or *"sons of the Covenant."* Paul is letting the Roman believers *(Jews and Gentiles)* know that there is *no partiality with God.* The Jew is not exempt from punishment. God has a plan for Israel that will be fulfilled, but when it comes to individual judgment, *there is no respect of persons with God.*

> **Romans 2:12 -** ***For as many as have sinned without law shall also perish without law: and as many as have sinned in the law shall be judged by the law;***

The Jew and Gentile are subject to divine wrath *here and now,* and in the *future judgment.* The Christian community in Rome had immature believers who were still wrestling with the scriptures concerning the Law and Gentile salvation. Try to imagine the conversations that many of the Jewish converts were having with the Gentiles. Paul is stressing to them that the Mosaic Law will not rescue the Jews from judgment because their own Law will judge them. The unbelieving Gentiles would be judged *without the Law.* Both must embrace Jesus as the Christ, the Son of God. While this may seem confusing to us now, Paul was writing to believers in Rome who had to look at a world around them that was filled with sin, and they had Christians in their community who were still studying the Torah while believing in Jesus. How did they reconcile the old sacrificial system and trusting in Jesus' death on the cross? Some of them were moral and immoral Jews who claimed to have the Law of Moses, and some were moral and immoral Gentiles without the Law of Moses.

While some scholars are on a theological collision course with Paul and pick and choose their verses trying to prove that salvation is by works, we have to compare and study the entire theme of what the *book of Romans* is saying. Paul will later address that all of the world is guilty before God and must come to faith in Christ to escape the judgment.

Romans 2:13 - *(For not the hearers of the law are just before God, but the doers of the law shall be justified.*

A religious Jew is not going to be saved from the judgment to come just because he has *heard* the Law or because he possesses a copy of the Law. Has the Jew kept the Law? No! The Gentile may think that because he does not have the Law that he will be saved in the end by good works. No! Humanity will be judged because all are sinners and all have broken God's Law. **(Romans 3:19-20)** Just because some people have kept part of the Law still does not merit everlasting life. The *book of James* makes it clear that if we have broken one point of the Law, we are guilty of the whole.

> ***For whosoever shall keep the whole law, and yet offend in one point, he is guilty of all.*** **James 2:10**

Jesus spoke about those who *heard* His words and did not do His words:

> ***Not every one that saith unto me, Lord, Lord, shall enter into the kingdom of heaven; but he that doeth the will of my Father which is in heaven.*** **Matthew 7:21**
>
> ***Therefore whosoever heareth these sayings of mine, and doeth them, I will liken him unto a wise man, which built his house upon a rock: And the rain descended, and the floods came, and the winds blew, and beat upon that house; and it fell not: for it was founded upon a rock. And every one that heareth these sayings of mine, and doeth them not, shall be likened unto a foolish man, which built his house upon the sand: And the rain descended, and the floods came, and the winds blew, and beat upon that house; and it fell: and great was the fall of it.*** **Matthew 7:24-27**

Romans 2:14-15 - ***For when the Gentiles, which have not the law, do by nature the things contained in the law, these, having not the law, are a law unto themselves: Which shew the work of the law written in their hearts, their conscience also bearing witness, and their thoughts the mean while accusing or else excusing one another;)***

In the Greco-Roman world in which Paul lived, much like our culture today, there could be found non-Jewish societies that were living a good moral life. This is because God's natural law of right and wrong was written in their conscience. Someone could be living on a remote island and he still has a conscience, or a *law unto themselves.* Now, sadly our world has reached the point where many people have their *conscience* seared over and are violating God's natural laws without ever being convicted. In the Day of Judgment, their own *conscience* will be used against them:

Speaking lies in hypocrisy; having their conscience seared with a hot iron. **I Timothy 4:2**

People who are not even religious often discuss other people's good or bad behavior, while later condemning themselves by doing the same things. Man is so sinful that he can talk a good talk one day and break his own *conscience* the next. The words we say will even condemn us one day. These words of Jesus come to mind:

But I say unto you, That every idle word that men shall speak, they shall give account thereof in the

day of judgment. For by thy words thou shalt be justified, and by thy words thou shalt be condemned. **Matthew 12:36-37**

Another truth is that after we receive Christ, sometimes Satan will use our past to try to condemn us. Please note what the Apostle John would later write to Christians:

For if our heart condemn us, God is greater than our heart, and knoweth all things. **I John 3:20**

As we make our way through these difficult words of the educated Jewish Apostle Paul, we need to repeat that he is using different arguments to state that all of humanity, religious or irreligious, are guilty before God. What then should a Gentile Christian in Rome say to Jewish people who might claim that they merited special favor from God?

Romans 2:16 - ***In the day when God shall judge the secrets of men by Jesus Christ according to my gospel.***

On this day no man will escape God's punishment by claiming ignorance of His written Law, because God's internal revelation is in the conscience of every individual, and that is enough to condemn us all.

"The secrets of men will be judged by Jesus Christ!" There were some Jews who believed that only the Father alone would judge the world-*not even the Messiah.* But note what Jesus said:

For the Father judgeth no man, but hath committed all judgment unto the Son: **John 5:22**

"according to my gospel" **-** Paul knew the gospel belonged to Jesus Christ, but he was referring to *the gospel that he preached.* The gospel that Paul preached was not just a sideline topic or something interesting to preach about, it was the basis on how all of humanity will be judged. He did not want the Christians in Rome to be influenced by the pagan philosophy around them. The gospel of Jesus Christ would be the ultimate standard on how sinful man would be judged.

The Boasting of the Jew

> **Romans 2:17 -** ***Behold, thou art called a Jew, and restest in the law, and makest thy boast of God,***

The boasting of the Jew is because of his possession of the Law. Instead of being humbled because God chose them as the nation to give the Law, they were extremely proud and confident. They believed that this confirmed their status as not only a chosen people, but ensured their salvation.

> **Romans 2:18-20 -** ***And knowest his will, and approvest the things that are more excellent, being instructed out of the law; And art confident that thou thyself art a guide of the blind, a light of them which are in darkness, An instructor of the foolish, a teacher of babes, which hast the form of knowledge and of the truth in the law.***

The Jewish Paul knew his own people and his own personal career as a Pharisee. **(Phil.3: 5)** He knew the religious pretense that marked the strictest sects of the Jews. The religious

Jew had *confidence* in his capacity to help the Gentiles who were in *darkness.* Paul mentions three areas of prideful self-esteem for the Jew:

- ***You know His will from the Law***
- ***You are instructed out of the Law***
- ***You have a form of knowledge and of the truth in the Law***

While God's will was formulated and embodied in the sacred Scriptures that contained the Law, the religious Jew was being self-righteous because God elected him. He was only *hearing* the Law, not *doing* the Law. The Jews were no more righteous than the Gentiles.

> **Romans 2:21-23 - *Thou therefore which teachest another, teachest thou not thyself? thou that preachest a man should not steal, dost thou steal? Thou that sayest a man should not commit adultery, dost thou commit adultery? thou that abhorrest idols, dost thou commit sacrilege? Thou that makest thy boast of the law, through breaking the law dishonourest thou God?***

What about the Jews' performance? Their confidence and pride did not match up with their actions. Paul is saying *"How can the Jew teach others but not oneself?"* The sins of *stealing* and *adultery* were very familiar sins that many of the Jews were committing, but what about the third sin, *sacrilege*?" Paul may have been referring to some of the Jews who stole property from the Gentiles which included pagan idols and then would resell the land for a profit.

The Jews claimed to despise pagan idols but would gain financial profit from hypocritical worship. One tradition they had was called *Corban,* where they would refuse to honor their father and mother saying that the money had been dedicated to the Temple. The Pharisees claimed to be leading people to the God of Israel and upholding His Law while being lovers of money. These verses are coming from the words of Jesus:

> ***For Moses said, Honour thy father and thy mother; and, Whoso curseth father or mother, let him die the death: But ye say, If a man shall say to his father or mother, It is Corban, that is to say, a gift, by whatsoever thou mightest be profited by me; he shall be free. And ye suffer him no more to do ought for his father or his mother; Making the word of God of none effect through your tradition, which ye have delivered: and many such like things do ye.*** **Mark 7:10-13**

> ***No servant can serve two masters: for either he will hate the one, and love the other; or else he will hold to the one, and despise the other. Ye cannot serve God and mammon. And the Pharisees also, who were covetous, heard all these things: and they derided him.*** **Luke 16:13-14**

> **Romans 2:24-25** - ***For the name of God is blasphemed among the Gentiles through you, as it is written. For circumcision verily profiteth, if thou keep the law: but if thou be a breaker of the law, thy circumcision is made uncircumcision.***

Paul was probably thinking about scriptures like **Isa. 52:5** and **Ezek. 36:22,** where God told Israel it had blasphemed His name among the heathen. In the Hebrew language, the profaning of God's name was called - *chilul ha-Shem.*

For the first time within this subunit Paul mentions *circumcision*; that not only represented the religious Jew, but also stood for his commitment to the Jewish Law.

> ***For I testify again to every man that is circumcised, that he is a debtor to do the whole law.*** **Galatians 5:3**

Circumcision avails nothing if the Jew does not keep the whole Law, and his religious status is reduced to that of the *uncircumcised* Gentiles. This brings us to the overall theme that Paul is expressing that the whole world is guilty before a holy God. Many Jews were trusting in *circumcision* for their relationship to God. But note a verse from the Torah and from *Galatians*:

> ***Cursed be he that confirmeth not all the words of this law to do them. And all the people shall say, Amen.*** **Deut. 27:26**
>
> ***For as many as are of the works of the law are under the curse: for it is written, Cursed is every one that continueth not in all things which are written in the book of the law to do them.*** **Galatians 3:10**

To prove the importance of the word ⋆*circumcision*, the Holy Bible mentions four kinds of *uncircumcision* with reference to man:

- ★ ***Uncircumcision of the ear*** **– Jeremiah 6:10**
- ★ ***Uncircumcision of lips*** **- Exodus 6:12**
- ★ ***Uncircumcision of the heart*** **– Deut. 10:16, Jeremiah 9:26**
- ★ ***Uncircumcision of the flesh*** **– Genesis 17:14**

★ *(Many Gentiles today replaced circumcision as the outward sign of their relationship to God with water baptism. This started with the Catholic Church and also during the Reformation Period. The same principle applies; unless the heart of the person is right with Jesus, the outward sign means nothing.)*

> **Romans 2:26-27 -** ***Therefore if the uncircumcision keep the righteousness of the law, shall not his uncircumcision be counted for circumcision? And shall not uncircumcision which is by nature, if it fulfil the law, judge thee, who by the letter and circumcision dost transgress the law?***

If an *uncircumcised* Gentile could keep the righteousness of the Law, then he could judge the *circumcised* Jew who does not keep the righteousness of the Law. Jesus gave a similar comparison with the *Queen of Sheba* and the *Ninevites* whom would someday judge the religious Jews of His day:

> ***The queen of the south shall rise up in the judgment with the men of this generation, and condemn them: for she came from the utmost parts of the earth to hear the wisdom of Solomon; and, behold, a greater than Solomon is here. The men of Nineve shall rise up in the judgment with this generation, and shall condemn***

> ***it: for they repented at the preaching of Jonas; and, behold, a greater than Jonas is here.*** **Luke 11:31-32**
>
> **Romans 2:28-29 -** ***For he is not a Jew, which is one outwardly; neither is that circumcision, which is outward in the flesh: But he is a Jew, which is one inwardly; and circumcision is that of the heart, in the spirit, and not in the letter; whose praise is not of men, but of God.***

It is interesting that Paul mentions the *praise of men* and the *praise of God.* The Hebrew word for Jew, *Yehudi*, means *"the one who praises."* **(Gen. 29:35, 49:8)** So the Jew, more so than any other person, should be the one who is giving *praise to God* for sending Christ into the world. Paul is warning them that if they are trusting in *circumcision* and the letter of the Law, they are not true, spiritual Jews.

The source of one's *praise* is crucial; will it come from men or from God? The only way that a Jew or a Gentile can receive *praise* from God is to be *circumcised in the spirit, or in the heart.* The zealous Jew might receive the *praise* he drew from men, like the Pharisees in Jesus' time, but this was nothing more than empty human glory. Paul shoots a final arrow to the observant Jew that if he knew his own heart, he would turn to Christ for salvation. The bottom line is that the Jew and the Gentile have *uncircumcised hearts* until they are born again and the Holy Spirit comes to live inside their hearts. On judgment day God will show no partiality to the unbelieving, religious Jew! A Jew or Gentile must be saved the same way through faith in Jesus the Christ, the Son of God!

CHAPTER THREE

What Advantage Does the Jew Have?

Romans 3:1-2 - ***What advantage then hath the Jew? or what profit is there of circumcision? Much every way: chiefly, because that unto them were committed the oracles of God.***

Paul has carefully explained in **Romans 2** that the possession of the Law or *circumcision* will not save a Jewish person. So what is the *advantage* of being a Jew? Paul says *much every way*! God gave the nation of Israel an indescribable gift, *the oracles of God.* The Greek word for *oracles* is *logia,* which means *"a statement originating from God."* **(Read Acts 7:38, Hebrews 5:12, I Peter 4:11)** A Jewish Paul is writing this epistle to the Romans. God gave his heavenly treasures, His library, and His declarations into the keeping of the ★ Jews.

★ *(While Paul is basically referring to the Old Testament scriptures, some scholars debate whether Luke was a Gentile, who penned the Gospel of Luke. This author believes that Luke was also a Jew.)*

Romans 3:3-4 - ***For what if some did not believe? shall their unbelief make the faith of God without effect?***

> ***God forbid: yea, let God be true, but every man a liar; as it is written, That thou mightest be justified in thy sayings, and mightest overcome when thou art judged.***

The fact that most of the Jews rejected Christ even until this day does not mean that God's faithfulness to them was in vain. The Gentile Christians in Rome were facing fierce opposition from some of the *unbelieving* Jews. The problem of the Jews not believing in Jesus as their Messiah was a problem of unbelief in their own scriptures. Jesus made this clear in several places:

> ***Search the scriptures; for in them ye think ye have eternal life: and they are they which testify of me.*** **John 5:39**

> ***For had ye believed Moses, ye would have believed me; for he wrote of me.*** **John 5:46**

Paul will discuss in **Romans 9-11** that God has not rejected His people. His promises to the nation of Israel have not been abandoned.

"God forbid" - Paul uses this *strong*, unusual phrase in several places throughout this epistle. **(Romans 3:6, 6:2, 6:15, 7:7, 7:13, 9:14, 11:1, 11:11)** This is a perfect example that the *book of Romans* has a Hebrew and Jewish background. How so? Paul was writing to a Greek-speaking community, but his Jewish background came out through many of his words and phrases. This phrase is a Hebrew *idiom*, called *chalilah*, which can mean *"far be it"* or *"God forbid."* It is used at least a dozen times in the Old Testament. **(Gen.44:7, 44:17, Joshua 22:29, 24:16, I Samuel 12:23, 14:45, 20:2, 24:6, 26:11, I Kings 21:3, I Chronicles 11:19, Job 27:5)**

It is even translated in places such as **Matthew 16:22** and **Luke 20:16.**

If God says one thing and every man in the world does another, God is still true. It is man that is the *liar,* not God, and He will be faithful to what He has promised. Though the nation of Israel did not believe and even caused the Gentiles not to believe, God would still be *justified* in His words. While it may sound strange and mysterious to us, the same scriptures that the Jewish people disregard will be ultimately fulfilled in their future blessing.

> ***"That thou mightest be justified in thy sayings, and mightest overcome when thou art judged."*** - David wrote about his own sin and God being justified:
>
> ***Against thee, thee only, have I sinned, and done this evil in thy sight: that thou mightest be justified when thou speakest, and be clear when thou judgest.*** **Psalm 51:4**
>
> **Romans 3:5-6** - ***But if our unrighteousness commend the righteousness of God, what shall we say? Is God unrighteous who taketh vengeance? (I speak as a man) God forbid: for then how shall God judge the world?***

Even though Paul says that he *speaks as a man,* he is still inspired by the Holy Spirit to write these words. Someone might say, *"How can God judge the world if He gave man the evil inclination to sin?"* Or how can *our unrighteousness commend the righteousness of God?* This is better understood with a couple of illustrations: one outside of the Bible and one within the inspiration of the sacred scriptures.

An exquisite diamond appears much more beautiful against a black background. One cannot see all of the many facets of a diamond on a light background. The black sinfulness of man brings out the pure righteousness of God.

What about ★ Judas Iscariot, one of Jesus' own disciples? Might Judas say, *"Lord, how can you judge me when you used me to fulfill the scriptures? If I had not betrayed Jesus, He would not have gone to the cross."* The answer is a profound yes! God used Judas' wickedness to fulfill the scriptures, and God knew what Judas was going to do. Judas was still guilty and deserves no credit for his wickedness; he is still responsible for his evil heart. It does not take away from God's righteousness just because a sinful person is unrighteous! A righteous God has every right to judge an unrighteous world! We will look more into this thought when we reach **Romans 5.**

★ (Study Psalm 41:9, John 13:18, Acts 1:16-17)

Romans 3:7-8 - *For if the truth of God hath more abounded through my lie unto his glory; why yet am I also judged as a sinner? And not rather, (as we be slanderously reported, and as some affirm that we say,) Let us do evil, that good may come? whose damnation is just.*

Because Paul preached that salvation was not by works but through faith in Jesus, some had *slanderously* accused him of giving people a right to sin in order that *God's glory* would be revealed. Paul states that those who believe this lie, *their damnation is just.* This idea of twisting God's glorious gift of eternal salvation, which gives us the faith and motivation to live a holy life for Christ, is worse than many of the pagans in Rome at that time. It is beyond the sin of the moralist and the self-righteousness of the religious Jew.

The Final Verdict

> **Romans 3:9 - *What then? are we better than they? No, in no wise: for we have before proved both Jews and Gentiles, that they are all under sin;***

Notice that Paul uses the pronoun *we* to include himself along with other Jews. By nature the Jew is no more right with God than the pagan or the Gentile moralist. *All are under sin and condemnation.* Every human being is under the tyrant ruler of sin. The reason for going to the extreme to show man's guilt before a holy God is for the Jews and Gentiles to realize they are spiritually lost and in need of a Savior. No one will fill a ★ need to come to Christ until he understands the holiness of God and the sinfulness of man.

★ *("Before I can preach love, mercy, and grace, I must preach sin, Law, and judgment. Preach 90% Law and 10% grace. I felt I did trust in Christ, Christ alone for salvation, and an assurance was given me that he had taken away my sins, even mine, and saved me from the law of sin and death." John Wesley, 1738, 24 May)*

> **Romans 3:10-18 - *As it is written, There is none righteous, no, not one: There is none that understandeth, there is none that seeketh after God. They are all gone out of the way, they are together***

> ***become unprofitable; there is none that doeth good, no, not one. Their throat is an open sepulchre; with their tongues they have used deceit; the poison of asps is under their lips: Whose mouth is full of cursing and bitterness: Their feet are swift to shed blood: Destruction and misery are in their ways: And the way of peace have they not known: There is no fear of God before their eyes.***

Paul uses the Old Testament to take a universal X-ray study into the life of a lost sinner. He uses a series of scripture to give the ultimate proof--the Word of God. **(Psalm 5:9, 10:7, 14:1-3, 53:1-3, 140:3, Eccl. 7:20, Isa. 59:7-8, Prov. 1:16)**

A few sins of commission and sins of omission are mentioned, but the sweeping reality is that there is *none righteous, no not one*! Man is so sinful that he *does not even seek after God* his Creator. Even when God sees the motive behind the so-called good deeds, the empty hypocrisy when man tries to worship God: *there is none that doeth good, no not one.* Man is *unprofitable* and the idea is that of rotten fruit. The *throat, the tongue, the lips, the mouth,* and *the feet* of man are all filled with sin and rebellion. Wherever there is sin, there is *no fear of God.*

> **Romans 3:19-20 -** ***Now we know that what things soever the law saith, it saith to them who are under the law: that every mouth may be stopped, and all the world may become guilty before God. Therefore by the deeds of the law there shall no flesh be justified in his sight: for by the law is the knowledge of sin.***

This description of man's sinfulness comes to us from the Law of God that was written centuries before. In Paul's day the religious Jews would take the Law and use it to condemn the Gentiles, not themselves. Paul makes it clear that God is speaking first to the Jews who are *under the law.* If God speaks this way to His chosen people who had the Law, it is evident that *by the deeds of the law no flesh will be justified in his sight.* The Law was given to show everyone *the knowledge of sin.* Since the days of Adam and Eve, sinful man has tried to use the fig leaves of religion to cover his sin and has failed. Hypothetically, if someone could start now and perfectly keep the Law, it would not make up for the past years of disobedience.

The end result is that sinful man *cannot even open his mouth* and is left without the capacity to counter the condemnation. We can be sure that the Jewish Paul never thought he would say such negative things about his brethren, but he left all of his previous Jewish perspectives back on the *Damascus Road.* Since he had found Christ and had been called to take the gospel to the Gentiles, he was a transformed man from the inside out. His view of the sacred scriptures and the holiness of God had been revolutionized.

Because of man's condemnation under the Law and because there is *none righteous no not one,* man should be prepared for God's provision. Is it possible for man to find a solution for his hopeless condition?

The Revelation of God's Righteousness

Romans 3:21-22 - *But now the righteousness of God without the law is manifested, being witnessed*

by the law and the prophets; Even the righteousness of God which is by faith of Jesus Christ unto all and upon all them that believe: for there is no difference:

These words provide the most glorious transition from the wrath and the judgment of God to the deliverance and the ★ *righteousness of God. But now* speaks of the newness of the work that God has provided *through* faith in the Lord Jesus Christ, which is really the New Covenant, with a continuity of what God started in the Old Testament. Since the Law was given to show man of his sinfulness, God designed a plan that would save lost humanity apart from the Law, apart from our own earning or deserving righteousness. The righteousness of God *through* the Messiah was predicted long ago and *witnessed by the law and the prophets.* The righteousness through Jesus Christ is not something that is a supplement of our own righteousness or good deeds, but *apart from the Law.* The Law was given to the Jews, but now the righteousness of God is given *through faith* in Christ to any *Jew or Gentile* who believes in Jesus. God's perfect righteousness is now available. Wow!

★ *(One of the titles of God in the Old Testament is "Yehovah Tsidkenu," the Lord our Righteousness.* **Jeremiah 23:5-6.** *The name of the capital city where God's people will live eternally is where the Lord is; wherein dwelleth righteousness.* **Ezekiel 48:35, 2 Peter 3:11-18, Revelation 21-22)**

There are those who think that because they have *faith,* they are being saved on the merit of their *faith.* But God's righteousness comes through faith in Jesus Christ and His finished work. Faith sees what God has already done through

His Son Jesus and believes God's Word. We can visibly see the *unrighteousness* that is in the world, but we have to obtain God's *righteousness* through the eyes of faith. It is so easy for us sinful humans to want credit for something instead of simply relying completely on who Christ is and what He has done for us. There are not many different gospels; there is only one gospel, one cure for man's sins, the blood and righteousness of God through Jesus Christ!

> **Romans 3:23-24 - *For all have sinned, and come short of the glory of God; Being justified freely by his grace through the redemption that is in Christ Jesus:***

God does not mention different categories of men's particular sins here. He just states that *all have sinned, and come short of the glory of God.* The fact that all of us are sinners is sufficient to condemn all of mankind. If we *all* have come short of God's glory, then *all* are in need of redemption. The religious, the irreligious, the moral, the immoral, the Jew or Gentile, all can *be justified freely by God's grace through the redemption that is in Christ Jesus.* The man standing on top of Mt. Everest or the man standing at the lowest point on planet earth, the Dead Sea, neither can touch the stars of heaven. Everyone is a sinner, but everyone can be *justified through Christ,* and it is *free*! Hallelujah!

> ***...., freely ye have received, freely give.* Matthew 10:8b**
>
> ***And the Spirit and the bride say, Come. And let him that heareth say, Come. And let him that is athirst***

> ***come. And whosoever will, let him take the water of life freely.*** **Revelation 22:17**

The Greek word for *"freely"* in this verse is *"dorean"* and it means *"something freely done, unearned and undeserved."* Notice this verse:

> ***But this cometh to pass, that the word might be fulfilled that is written in their law, They hated me <u>without a cause</u>*** *(dorean)*. **John 15:25**

There was nothing in Jesus that deserved the hatred of man; therefore, there is nothing within us that is deserving of His justification - all reasons come from the love of God. Ministers of the gospel of Christ need to realize that we have been called to take the message that can give anyone eternal life, the most important message in the universe. And we need to be reminded that while it is free to us, it cost Jesus Christ His precious blood when He died on the tree. It is sad how the gospel has been turned into a lucrative business. We must separate God's kingdom work from the mind of the secular world. In the qualifications of being a leader in the church, he must not be *greedy of filthy lucre.* **(I Timothy 3:3)** This is why the Apostle Paul would later write these words about his desire not to hinder the gospel by receiving carnal things:

> ***For though I preach the gospel, I have nothing to glory of: for necessity is laid upon me; yea, woe is unto me, if I preach not the gospel! For if I do this thing willingly, I have a reward: but if against my will, a dispensation of the gospel is committed unto me. What is my reward then? Verily that, when I***

> ***preach the gospel, I may make the gospel of Christ without charge, that I abuse not my power in the gospel.* I Corinthians 9:16-18**

"the redemption that is in Christ Jesus" **-** The Greek word here for *redemption* is *apolutrosis*, and it means *"to buy back."* While salvation is free to us, God paid the cost by giving the world His only Son. He *bought us back from the slavery of sin* through the blood of His Son Jesus. Jesus is the New Testament ⋆ *Kinsman-Redeemer.*

⋆ *While Yahweh is Israel's Redeemer in the Old Testament, a beautiful illustration of the Kinsman-Redeemer is the Book of Ruth, where Boaz redeems the poor and needy Ruth, the Moabite.* **(Ruth 3:9, Matt. 1:5)** *A Kinsman-Redeemer had to be a relative, and Jesus was not ashamed to call us His brethren.* **(Hebrews 2:11)**

Later on Paul would use these words in describing why a Christian should live a holy life:

> ***For ye are bought with a price: therefore glorify God in your body, and in your spirit, which are God's.* I Corinthians 6:20**

God Displays His Mercy-Seat

> **Romans 3:25 - *Whom God hath set forth to be a propitiation through faith in his blood, to declare his righteousness for the remission of sins that are past, through the forbearance of God;***

This verse is so powerful that we need to make the correlation with the Hebrew Scriptures. The Greek word here for *propitiation* is *hilasterion*, and it means *"lid of the mercy seat."* The connection goes back to the Hebrew word, *kaporet*, where the blood of the sacrificial animals was sprinkled as the atonement for the sins of Israel.

> ***And make one cherub on the one end, and the other cherub on the other end: even of the mercy seat*** *(kaporet)* ***shall ye make the cherubims on the two ends thereof.*** **Exodus 25:19**
>
> ***And he shall take of the blood of the bullock, and sprinkle it with his finger upon the mercy seat*** *(kaporet)* ***eastward; and before the mercy seat*** *(kaporet)* ***shall he sprinkle of the blood with his finger seven times. Then shall he kill the goat of the sin offering, that is for the people, and bring his blood within the vail, and do with that blood as he did with the blood of the bullock, and sprinkle it upon the mercy seat,*** *(kaporet)* ***and before the mercy seat*** *(kaporet)****:*** **Leviticus 16:14-15**

In typology, Jesus functions as the *Mercy Seat,* where a holy God and sinful man can meet together. Jesus was not just appeasing a vengeful God who was unwilling to hold back His wrath, but it was God setting Him forth on display on the cross.

"through faith in his blood, to declare his righteousness for the remission of sins that are past, through the forbearance of God;" This phrase is used only once in Paul's writings, showing how important the blood of Jesus really is. How can a holy and righteous God meet with sinful humanity? It is only when someone places faith ***in*** the blood of Jesus Christ!

For the saints in the Old Testament, *God in His forbearance, passed over their sins with the sacrifices,* but on the cross, the blood of Jesus paid for their sins. All of those sacrifices in the Old Covenant were looking forward to their fulfillment in the Messiah's blood. This is the glorious truth when the veil of the Temple was rent when Jesus died on the tree:

> ***And, behold, the veil of the temple was rent in twain from the top to the bottom; and the earth did quake, and the rocks rent;*** **Matthew 27:51**

> **Romans 3:26 -** ***To declare, I say, at this time his righteousness: that he might be just, and the justifier of him which believeth in Jesus.***

This is a glorious truth and should bring tears of joy to the reader! Justice and mercy met at the cross! Not only did the blood of Jesus provide proof of *God's righteousness* for the sins in ages past, but also of vindicating *His righteousness* at the present time. With one arm Jesus reached out to atone for the sins of the saints in the Old Testament, and with the other arm He reached out to the sins of the saints in the New Testament. Truly the words of John the Baptist are seen more clearly in this verse:

> ***The next day John seeth Jesus coming unto him, and saith, Behold the Lamb of God, which taketh away the sin of the world.*** **John 1:29**

Through the precious blood of Christ, *God is just and holy and can still justify the guilty sinner.* It is all through *faith in Jesus*! After the coming of the Hebrew *Yeshua*, or the English

Jesus, into the world, it was no longer adequate to believe in a Messiah whose identity was not known. Notice these verses:

> ***Neither is there salvation in any other: for there is none other name under heaven given among men, whereby we must be saved.*** **Acts 4:12**
>
> ***Wherefore God also hath highly exalted him, and given him a name which is above every name: That at the name of Jesus every knee should bow, of things in heaven, and things in earth, and things under the earth; And that every tongue should confess that Jesus Christ is Lord, to the glory of God the Father.*** **Philippians 2:9-11**

Theologians have spilled a tremendous amount of ink over the centuries trying to twist Paul's words and randomly pick and choose a verse out of context, trying to prove that sinful man is justified by his faith in Christ *plus* good works. Good works either under the Law of Moses or after the Law are still *works*. In the New Testament there is a direct opposite between *grace and works*. The soteriology of the Protestant Reformation *(The movement in the 1500's that broke away from the Catholic Church)* denied good works to enter the door of salvation but that reintroduced good works through the back door. This is one reason why there are so many different Christian denominations in the world today. Note what Paul said in his book to the Galatians:

> ***I do not frustrate the grace of God: for if righteousness come by the law, then Christ is dead in vain.*** **Galatians 2:21**

Romans 3:27 - *Where is boasting then? It is excluded. By what law? of works? Nay: but by the law of faith.*

There is no place for self-congratulations or any credit on man's part. ★ *Boasting* is excluded in the *law of faith*! The Jew cannot boast of his righteousness over the Gentiles. This is why so many do not like to study about being justified freely by God's grace because it does not give any room for his sinful pride.

★ *(Many professing Christians have lost their identity in Christ. They still boast about being a member of a certain church, or boast about their Christian education, or boast about their faithfulness to their religious heritage, or their baptism, or their catechism, or boast about their ancestry. God designed the plan of salvation, not prideful, sinful man.)*

Romans 3:28-29 - *Therefore we conclude that a man is justified by faith without the deeds of the law. Is he the God of the Jews only? is he not also of the Gentiles? Yes, of the Gentiles also:*

The conclusion is that sinful man is not justified *by faith plus the deeds of the Law but we are justified without the deeds of the Law.* In the *book of James* the *character* of biblical faith is discussed. **(James 2:17-26)** Theologians and ministers still have problems reconciling what Paul is saying in Romans with the *book of James.* Paul is setting forth how a sinful man is justified and how he receives a righteous standing before a holy God, while James is stating how man proves he has been justified.

The plan of salvation is universal for everyone. There is not one plan of salvation for the Jew and another for the Gentile. Many times in the Old Testament the words used for the

Gentiles were names such as: *sojourner, stranger, nations.* Notice these verses that mention the *Gentiles* and how they connect to Jesus and why Paul mentions the Jews *and* Gentiles so often:

> ***I the Lord have called thee in righteousness, and will hold thine hand, and will keep thee, and give thee for a covenant of the people, for a light of the Gentiles;*** **Isaiah 42:6**

> ***Arise, shine; for thy light is come, and the glory of the Lord is risen upon thee. For, behold, the darkness shall cover the earth, and gross darkness the people: but the Lord shall arise upon thee, and his glory shall be seen upon thee. And the Gentiles shall come to thy light, and kings to the brightness of thy rising.*** **Isaiah 60:1-3**

> ***For mine eyes have seen thy salvation, Which thou hast prepared before the face of all people; A light to lighten the Gentiles, and the glory of thy people Israel.*** **Luke 2:30-32**

> **Romans 3:30-31** - ***Seeing it is one God, which shall justify the circumcision by faith, and uncircumcision through faith. Do we then make void the law through faith? God forbid: yea, we establish the law.***

Knowing that there is only *one God,* He always cared for the rest of the world even though He gave the Jews a special calling and purpose. For example, notice how God showed special care over the Land of Israel.

> ***A land which the Lord thy God careth for: the eyes of the Lord thy God are always upon it, from the beginning of the year even unto the end of the year.*** **Deut. 11:12**
>
> ***To cause it to rain on the earth, where no man is; on the wilderness, wherein there is no man; To satisfy the desolate and waste ground; and to cause the bud of the tender herb to spring forth?*** **Job 38:26-27**

Not only is the righteousness of God available to the *circumcision* (Jews) and the *uncircumcision* (Gentiles) through faith, it is also received the same way. *By faith and through faith* means that God *justifies the Jew and Gentile* the same way.

As Paul will demonstrate in **Romans 4,** the Law was *established* through the gospel. The Law anticipated the coming of the Messiah of Israel to fulfill all of the sacrificial system. One of the great studies we can dive into is how Jesus the Messiah fulfilled all of the shadows and types in the Old Testament, and the 57 times in the New Testament it says, *"that the scriptures might be fulfilled."* One cannot understand Jesus being our *Great High Priest* until he carefully studies and compares the *book of Leviticus* with the *book of Hebrews.* While the Holy Bible is divided with the Old and New Testaments, it is one inspired piece of divine tapestry. That is why the gospel of Christ *establishes* the Law, and the seriousness of Jesus coming all the way from heaven to suffer the horrible death of crucifixion proves that the Law cannot be ignored.

> ***For even <u>Christ our passover</u> is sacrificed for us:*** **I Corinthians 5:7**

> ***Let no man therefore judge you in meat, or in drink, or in respect of an holyday, or of the new moon, or of the sabbath days: Which are a shadow of things to come; but the body is of Christ.*** **Colossians 2:16-17**

Notice that once again Paul uses the strong Hebrew style of writing called, *chalilah*, which means *"God forbid,"* or *"far be it"* that the Law is made void.

CHAPTER FOUR

Abraham is Declared Righteousness

> **Romans 4:1-3 -** ***What shall we say then that Abraham our father, as pertaining to the flesh, hath found? For if Abraham were justified by works, he hath whereof to glory; but not before God. For what saith the scripture? Abraham believed God, and it was counted unto him for righteousness.***

While *Abraham* is considered *the father* of the Jewish people, he was a Syrian from the land of Mesopotamia. **(Deut. 26:5)** No doubt there were Jews in Rome who had been converted to Christ and still argued that ⋆ *Abraham* received righteousness because he kept the Law. Because *Abraham* was not a natural Jew and he lived long before Moses was given the Law, Paul is building the argument that he started back in **Romans 3.** If *Abraham* received righteousness because of his works, then the *glory* would go to *Abraham.*

⋆ *(Ancient writings from some of the rabbis wrote, "We find our father Abraham had performed the whole Law before it was given.")*

"but not before God" **-** The problem goes on today in religious circles when we compare men to other men instead of comparing them to God. A person may look good in the eyes of others and think, *"I am a good person,"* because he has lived a better moral life than someone else. The only way that *Abraham* or anyone else can be declared righteous *before* a holy God is through faith in a righteous Savior. Even though *Abraham* lived centuries before Christ came into the world, the gospel was preached to *Abraham*:

> ***Your father Abraham rejoiced to see my day: and he saw it, and was glad. Then said the Jews unto him, Thou art not yet fifty years old, and hast thou seen Abraham? Jesus said unto them, Verily, verily, I say unto you, Before Abraham was, I am.*** **John 8:56-58**
>
> ***And the scripture, foreseeing that God would justify the heathen through faith, preached before the gospel unto Abraham, saying, In thee shall all nations be blessed.*** **Galatians 3:8**
>
> ***"Abraham believed God, and it was counted unto him for righteousness"***

Paul is quoting from **Genesis 15:6.** In Genesis the original Hebrew word for *"counted"* is *chashab*, and it means *"account, or determined." Abraham* was *determined* to be righteous not because he kept the Law or because he was circumcised, but because he simply *believed God.* It did not matter what others thought of *Abraham.* God placed him in a *righteous standing* in the *accounting* of Almighty God because of his faith.

There was a salvation promise in the initial call of *Abraham* to leave the land of *Ur of the Chaldees:*

> ***Now the Lord had said unto Abram, Get thee out of thy country, and from thy kindred, and from thy father's house, unto a land that I will shew thee: And I will make of thee a great nation, and I will bless thee, and make thy name great; and thou shalt be a blessing: And I will bless them that bless thee, and curse him that curseth thee: and in thee shall all families of the earth be blessed.*** **Genesis 12:1-3**

This *faith-righteousness* that was between a holy God and *Abraham* is the prototype for the experience of believers in all succeeding generations. Paul must have used this often in his synagogue sermons whenever he proclaimed Christ in the Roman world.

> **Romans 4:4-5** - ***Now to him that worketh is the reward not reckoned of grace, but of debt. * But to him that worketh not, but believeth on him that justifieth the ungodly, his faith is counted for righteousness.***

In God's accounting system, if Abraham had a *works-righteousness,* then he would have been placed in the *"earned pay column."* Because Abraham had *faith-righteousness,* he belongs in the *"unearned gift column."* Jesus died on the cross for the people who hated Him, so the gift of salvation is all of grace!

Righteousness is given to those who believe, not for those who think they can be justified by living a good life of works. Because of the offering of Christ on the cross, God can *justify the ungodly*. This is not promoting laziness, or to think that God is happy about our ungodliness, but it shows the miracle of God's love and mercy toward sinners. The supernatural miracle of grace is why so many people stumble over God's gift of salvation; they still think they can work for it. While the New Testament saints have *benefits* of salvation that the Old Testament saints did not have, we do not have a different *manner* of salvation.

★ *(There was an old preacher man who this author knew that quoted this verse on many occasions when meeting together on hospital visits. While other preachers would quote more familiar verses, this old preacher loved this one particular verse. Because of his passion for this verse, this author has always remembered the truth it holds.)*

> **Romans 4:6-8 - *Even as David also describeth the blessedness of the man, unto whom God imputeth righteousness without works, Saying, Blessed are they whose iniquities are forgiven, and whose sins are covered. Blessed is the man to whom the Lord will not impute sin.***

While this requires some deeper thinking, Paul uses a Hebrew principle called *gezerah shavah,* or *verbal analogy,* where the same Hebrew verb *chashab* that is used in **Genesis 15:6** for *"counted,"* is used in **Psalm 32** where David links the verb to a *blessing.* ***Blessed is he whose transgression is forgiven, whose sin is covered. Blessed is the man unto whom the Lord imputeth*** *(chashab)* ***not iniquity, and in whose spirit there is no guile.*** **Psalm 32:1-2**

David is writing about *blessedness* of one who is not justified through works. *David* knew very well about his sins, and yet he was *blessed* and cleansed through the divine work of *imputation* in a different sense than *Abraham*, but the same principle applies. His sins were not *imputed (chashab)* unto him, and therefore *David was blessed.*

Righteousness Is Apart From Ordinances

> **Romans 4:9-12 - *Cometh this blessedness then upon the circumcision only, or upon the uncircumcision also? for we say that faith was reckoned to Abraham for righteousness. How was it then reckoned? when he was in circumcision, or in uncircumcision? Not in circumcision, but in uncircumcision. And he received the sign of circumcision, a seal of the righteousness of the faith which he had yet being uncircumcised: that he might be the father of all them that believe, though they be not circumcised; that righteousness might be imputed unto them also: And the father of circumcision to them who are not of the circumcision only, but who also walk in the steps of that faith of our father Abraham, which he had being yet uncircumcised.***

The *blessing* that *David* enjoyed by knowing his sins were forgiven, and the *righteousness* that *Abraham* was given was not based upon *circumcision* or any ordinance. *Abraham* was counted for righteousness in **Genesis 15:6,** and he did not receive the covenant of circumcision until **Genesis 17.** *Abraham* was declared righteous while he was still *uncircumcised* to show that not only the Jews, but also the Gentiles can be *children of Abraham* by believing in Christ.

> ***Even as Abraham believed God, and it was accounted to him for righteousness. Know ye therefore that they which are of faith, the same are the children of Abraham.* Galatians 3:6-7**
>
> ***That the blessing of Abraham might come on the Gentiles through Jesus Christ; that we might receive the promise of the Spirit through faith.* Galatians 3:14**

To be a true child of *Abraham*, he must come by faith in Jesus who died on the cross. What is astounding is that the covenant God made with *Abraham* in *Genesis* is still in effect today *without the Law or without any ordinance* because the death of Jesus provides righteousness to us through faith.

> ***Christ hath redeemed us from the curse of the law, being made a curse for us: for it is written, Cursed is every one that hangeth on a tree:* Galatians 3:13**

In Paul's day the Gentiles who wanted to convert to the faith of the God of Israel had to be *circumcised*, and they could not call Abraham *"our father."* Paul throws out that distinction and says that everyone who comes to faith in Jesus can say *"our father Abraham."* Think what a shock this must have been to the Jewish believers in Rome to hear these words for the very first time. They had to have *Abraham's faith, not his circumcision,* to have righteousness. Because *Abraham* would become the father of *all* people who believe in Christ, it caused God to change his name.

The breath of *Yahweh* breathed upon *Abram* and added His breath in his name:

> ***Abram; the same is Abraham.*** **I Chronicles 1:27**

Paul picks up the metaphor that is suggested where God tells Abraham that He will make his descendants as innumerable as the dust of the earth. In the world to come, the population will be all of the descendants of *Abraham*, both Jews and Gentiles.

> ***And I will make thy seed as the dust of the earth: so that if a man can number the dust of the earth, then shall thy seed also be numbered.*** **Genesis 13:16**

The Promise to Abraham's Seed is By Faith

> **Romans 4:13-15** - ***For the promise, that he should be the heir of the world, was not to Abraham, or to his seed, through the law, but through the righteousness of faith. For if they which are of the law be heirs, faith is made void, and the promise made of none effect: Because the law worketh wrath: for where no law is, there is no transgression.***

If Abraham and his seed received righteousness by the Law, then *faith is void and God's promise is of no effect.* God dealt with Abraham, Isaac, and Jacob before the Law was ever given. Faith is the ground of God's blessing! The reason the Law cannot bring anyone into the blessings of God is not because the Law is bad, but because no one can keep the Law. The *Law brings about wrath* if someone uses this principle to try to have a relationship with God. Sin is a violation of God's righteous standards whether the sinner realizes he has broken the Law or not. The presence of the Law confronts the sinner with the fact that his behavior is a *transgression* of God's will and therefore is subject to *wrath.*

> **Romans 4:16-18 - *Therefore it is of faith, that it might be by grace; to the end the promise might be sure to all the seed; not to that only which is of the law, but to that also which is of the faith of Abraham; who is the father of us all, (As it is written, I have made thee a father of many nations,) before him whom he believed, even God, who quickeneth the dead, and calleth those things which be not as though they were. Who against hope believed in hope, that he might become the father of many nations; according to that which was spoken, So shall thy seed be.***

Faith is related to grace the same way works are related to the Law. God's grace is appropriated by faith.

Paul may be referring to *Abraham's calling,* the supernatural birth of Isaac, the birth of the Jewish nation, and the power of God to bring *life from the dead.* He is probably alluding to the Gentiles who were not a people since they were dead in trespasses and sins, but are now saved by grace.

> ***And you hath he quickened, who were dead in trespasses and sins;*** **Ephesians 2:1**
>
> ***That at that time ye were without Christ, being aliens from the commonwealth of Israel, and strangers***

> ***from the covenants of promise, having no hope, and without God in the world:*** **Ephesians 2:12**

> ***Yet the number of the children of Israel shall be as the sand of the sea, which cannot be measured nor numbered; and it shall come to pass, that in the place where it was said unto them, Ye are not my people, there it shall be said unto them, Ye are the sons of the living God.*** **Hosea 1:10**

"So shall thy seed be" **-** This is another good example of how all of the sacred scriptures are connected. Even the promise of God to Abraham was a spiritual prototype of the salvation that would come to the Gentiles.

> ***And he brought him forth abroad, and said, Look now toward heaven, and tell the stars, if thou be able to number them: and he said unto him, So shall thy seed be.*** **Genesis 15:5**

Abraham's *hope* was to be the *father of many nations*, and it was all based upon God's promise. The fact that God would provide a son *(Isaac)* for Abraham and make him fruitful *physically* is paralleled by the hopelessness of the Gentiles, who would later be made children of Abraham *spiritually*. Wow!

> **Romans 4:19-21 -** ***And being not weak in faith, he considered not his own body now dead, when he was about an hundred years old, neither yet the deadness of Sarah's womb: He staggered not at the promise of God through unbelief; but was strong in faith, giving***

> ***glory to God; And being fully persuaded that, what he had promised, he was able also to perform.***

There is a saying in Hebrew called, *"ketanei 'emunah,"* which means *"small in faith,"* when people are only trusting in what they can see. Although Abraham's body was *dead* as far as communicating life by physical means, and *Sarah's womb was dead,* he did not look at his outward circumstances. Abraham did not waver at *the promise of God.* He was fully convinced that God was able to perform what He had promised. By taking God at His word, Abraham gave *glory to God*!

The words *"fully persuaded"* is one word in the Greek, *"plerophoreo"* and is seldom used in the New Testament. One place is the very first verse of Luke's gospel:

> ***Forasmuch as many have taken in hand to set forth in order a declaration of those things which are most surely believed*** *(plerophoreo)* ***among us.*** **Luke 1:1**

> **Romans 4:22-25** - ***And therefore it was imputed to him for righteousness. Now it was not written for his sake alone, that it was imputed to him; But for us also, to whom it shall be imputed, if we believe on him that raised up Jesus our Lord from the dead; Who was delivered for our offences, and was raised again for our justification.***

The *imputation of righteousness* was not because of Abraham's obedience, but because of his faith in God. It was not only for the benefit of Abraham that God declared him righteous through faith, but he was an example to everyone, Jew or Gentile, who believes that Jesus died and rose again. Paul is not treating the sacred Scriptures as a mere historical record, but as the timeless Word of God. When God declared Abraham righteous, He also was pointing ahead to Paul's day and to our present day. The record of Abraham's faith was intended to offer scriptural support to the proclamation about the finished work of Jesus the Son of God! Abraham believed in the very same God that we believe in today! The Old Testament does not contradict the gospel of salvation by grace through faith. Abraham being justified by faith and being given a righteous standing before a holy God by faith is our pattern.

"Who was delivered for our offences, and was raised again for our justification" - The word for "delivered" is the word *"paradidomi,"* and it means *"to hand over."* God the Father *handed over* Jesus deliberately for the sake of our *offences* so that Jesus could be raised again so we could be *justified*. Our *sins* necessitated the death of Christ, and our *justification* required His resurrection. This same Greek word is used in **Romans 8:32:**

He that spared not his own Son, but delivered him up *(paradidomi)* ***for us all, how shall he not with him also freely give us all things?***

It was all the work of God. *"Salvation belongs to the Lord."* **(Psalm 3:8)**

- ***Faith in the historical events of Jesus will not save us***
- ***Faith in the pure life of Jesus will not save us***
- ***Faith in the accuracy of Jesus' teaching will not save us***
- ***Faith in the miracles of Jesus will not save us***
- ***Only Faith in the death of Jesus on the cross, His burial, and His resurrection will save us***

The fact that God brought life from the deadness of Abraham and Sarah and brought Jesus forth from the grave connects us with the wonderful truth that God created a people *(the Gentiles)* who were *not a people.* The resurrection of Christ is the bridge that will connect us to **Romans 5-8** where Paul moves on to the implications of what this truth means for the Christian experience.

CHAPTER FIVE

Justification Brings Victory

Romans 5:1-2 - *Therefore being justified by faith, we have peace with God through our Lord Jesus Christ: By whom also we have access by faith into this grace wherein we stand, and rejoice in hope of the glory of God.*

While we were all found guilty in the court of God's law, God's glory, and even our own conscience, our guilty sentence has been transferred to a sentence of being *justified because of our faith in Jesus.* God is now satisfied, and the first benefit is that *we have peace with God through our Lord Jesus Christ.* This is peace *with God!* God has won the battle between holiness and sin. He won by *winning us.* This is also reiterated later in Paul's writing to the people of Ephesus in **Ephesians 2:14.** *Jesus is our peace*!

While life is still a battle with the devil, the world, the flesh, and with sin in our daily lives, the peace we have with God is settled! We are not battling *against* God, but *for* God. The second point of victory is that *we have access into the grace in which we stand.* Grace is not only the beginning principle, but we stand in God's grace and continue in His grace. Because we are in Jesus, we have *access* to this grace. The idea is that in the Old Testament the high priest had *access* to the Holy of Holies only once a year. **(Hebrews 9:7)** Because we have met a holy God through faith in the death of Christ on the cross, we can enter into God's grace anytime. Prayer is the obvious way in which we have access to His Divine presence:

> ***For we have not an high priest which cannot be touched with the feeling of our infirmities; but was in all points tempted like as we are, yet without sin. Let us therefore come boldly unto the throne of grace, that we may obtain mercy, and find grace to help in time of need.*** **(Hebrews 4:15-16)**

God did not give us righteousness just to give us an interview, but to remain with Him. We are a part of His family, and we can walk in His light everyday! So we have *peace with God,* and we have *access into the grace that saved us.*

Paul mentions something else, *we can rejoice in the hope of the glory of God.* When we consider all that God has done for us through Christ, we can walk triumphantly in the *abundant joy* of knowing that one day we will behold *God's glory* and be made into the image of Jesus the Christ! These words come to mind when Jesus was praying to the Father:

> ***I am come that they might have life, and that they might have it more abundantly.*** **John 10:10a**
>
> ***Father, I will that they also, whom thou hast given me, be with me where I am; that they may behold my***

glory, which thou hast given me: for thou lovedst me before the foundation of the world. **John 17:24**

Beloved, now are we the sons of God, and it doth not yet appear what we shall be: but we know that, when he shall appear, we shall be like him; for we shall see him as he is. **I John 3:2**

Glory in the Present Time

Romans 5:3-4 - ***And not only so, but we glory in tribulations also: knowing that tribulation worketh patience; And patience, experience; and experience, hope:***

Paul understood that *tribulations and suffering* were not necessarily a sign of God's displeasure, but a sign of His care. Tribulations are used by God to test our character, and therefore believers in Christ can *glory* in their trials and persecutions. *Glory* does not just apply to the sweet bye-and-bye, but to the present time. It is not through times of great blessings that we grow closer to our Lord, but through times of suffering. Paul seems to be reflecting on an actual situation that the early Christian community in Rome was going through. Paul was living out a life of hardships, and he knew this truth better than anyone.

Once a person comes to know the righteousness of God through faith in Christ, he comes to look at tribulations in a different light. Tribulations in the life of a follower of Christ are a part of the journey, like a sailor goes out to sea, or a soldier goes into battle. If someone is only a professing Christian, then tribulations will turn his life bitter and make him even more carnal. If someone is a born again believer in Jesus, tribulations will make him more powerful, wise, gentle, and humble. There is a golden chain in Christian growth and maturity: *tribulation, endurance, experience, and hope.* Someone who has gone through afflictions and sufferings as a follower of Christ can be used on the front lines of ministry. How can we help others go through troubles if we have not been there ourselves? In contrast, God's *wrath* is upon the unrighteous, while God's *approval* is upon the ones who are righteous and endure tribulations. David sang about this truth centuries ago:

> ***Oh let the wickedness of the wicked come to an end; but establish the just: for the righteous God trieth the hearts and reins.*** **Psalm 7:9**

The Apostle Peter would later write about the stepladder in climbing up to being a stronger believer in Jesus:

> ***And beside this, giving all diligence, add to your faith virtue; and to virtue knowledge; And to knowledge temperance; and to temperance patience; and to patience godliness; And to godliness brotherly kindness; and to brotherly kindness charity.*** **2 Peter 1:5-7**
>
> **Romans 5:5 -** ***And hope maketh not ashamed; because the love of God is shed abroad in our hearts by the Holy Ghost which is given unto us.***

Tribulation starts the process that brings hope to fruition. This hope *will not make us ashamed or disappoint us because the love of God has been shed abroad in our hearts by the Holy Ghost.* Some Christians live as though it was only a trickle when we were saved by His grace, but God wants us to know the *outpouring of His love* for us by giving us His Son Jesus. Not only does Paul desire for the believers in Rome to know how much God loves them, but he also wants them to know that God has entrusted them with the gospel to never be *ashamed* of Him.

Jesus Christ is our *righteousness, sanctification and redemption,* **(I Cor. 1:30)** He is *the glory of God,* **(Romans 3:23)** He is *the power and wisdom of God,* **(I Cor. 1:24)** and He is our hope:

> ***Paul, an apostle of Jesus Christ by the commandment of God our Saviour, and Lord Jesus Christ, which is <u>our hope</u>;*** **I Timothy 1:1**

A Description of God's Love For Us

> **Romans 5:6-8** - ***For when we were yet without strength, in due time Christ died for the ungodly. For scarcely for a righteous man will one die: yet peradventure for a good man some would even dare to die. But God commendeth his love toward us, in that, while we were yet sinners, Christ died for us.***

Before the whole process of salvation began, we were *without strength and helpless,* but God's solution to our profound weakness was to *send Christ to die in due time.* Christ died *for,* the Greek *huper,* the ungodly, which means *"on behalf of, for the sake of."* Notice these two verses where the same word is used:

> ***Nor consider that it is expedient for us, that one man should die for*** *(huper)* ***the people, and that the whole nation perish not.*** **John 11:50**

> ***Christ hath redeemed us from the curse of the law, being made a curse for** (huper) **us: for it is written, Cursed is every one that hangeth on a tree:*** **Galatians 3:13**

It was all done for our sakes! How deep and eternal is God's love for His children!

> ***May be able to comprehend with all saints what is the breadth, and length, and depth, and height; And to know the love of Christ, which passeth knowledge, that ye might be filled with all the fulness of God.*** **Ephesians 3:18-19**

While it may have seemed late for the remnant that was looking for Him, Jesus came precisely at the point in ⋆ human history that God had foreordained. **(Galatians 4:4)** Many times our Lord Jesus would say, *"The time is fulfilled."* **(Mark 1:15, Luke 4:19, Isaiah 61:1-2)** This was the starting point in which *weak and ungodly* people like us could become *spiritually strong* through the indwelling power of the Holy Spirit. Believers in Christ can now live with the heavenly joy that was founded upon God's love. We are no longer hopeless!

⋆ *(The world was prepared spiritually, economically, linguistically, politically, philosophically, and geographically for the coming of Jesus and the spread of the gospel. The believers in Rome were living in the city from where Rome thought they ruled the world. God used Rome to help spread the gospel and to show that God overrules in the affairs of man.)*

"For scarcely for a righteous man will one die: yet peradventure for a good man some would even dare to die" **-** A good man *might* die a noble death for the right kind of person.

A parent *might* die for one of his children, but Jesus died the horrible death of crucifixion on a tree for the unrighteous and ungodly. What a thought! Here Paul is contrasting human love from Divine love. A good biblical illustration is that Abraham interceded on behalf of the inhabitants of Sodom. **(Gen.18:22)** Moses interceded on behalf of the children of Israel. **(Exo.32:7)** Jesus Christ, the God-Man, died for Abraham's sins, Moses' sins, and the sins of all mankind.

"But God commendeth his love toward us, in that, while we were yet sinners, Christ died for us" **-** The starting point for us to realize God's great love for us is always the cross of Christ. God's love was on display when Jesus hung on the tree in Jerusalem. Notice this verse:

> ***To wit, that God was in Christ, reconciling the world unto himself, not imputing their trespasses unto them; and hath committed unto us the word of reconciliation.*** **2 Cor. 5:19**

The height of man's hatred cannot defeat the height of God's love. It is not only that Jesus died, but Jesus also died for undeserving sinners and those who rebel against Him.

Free From God's Wrath

> **Romans 5:9-11 -** ***Much more then, being now justified by his blood, we shall be saved from wrath through him. For if, when we were enemies, we were reconciled to God by the death of his Son, much more, being reconciled, we shall be saved by his life. And not***

> ***only so, but we also joy in God through our Lord Jesus Christ, by whom we have now received the atonement.***

While Paul is writing in Greek, we must remember that he is a Hebrew-speaking Jew, and the *Much more* here is a Hebrew style of teaching called *kal ve-chomer,* showing that we are saved and justified by the blood of Jesus. We are most assuredly saved from *the wrath of God* that will come upon all of those who reject Christ as their personal Savior. Jesus used this Hebrew style of teaching on several occasions. **(Matt. 6:30, 7:11)** It is true that we are saved from the world, the flesh, and the devil, but we are also rescued from *God's wrath* that is coming on the world. This is one of the most powerful verses in Paul's epistle to the Romans, and it is not just referring to the future wrath of God, but it touches our lives here and now. God may chasten us and correct us, but we have been set free from His wrath.

"For if, when we were enemies, we were reconciled to God by the death of his Son, much more, being reconciled, we shall be saved by his life." - If God showed such great love to us while we were His enemies, *how much more* are the blessings once we have been reconciled to God through Christ? If the death of Christ reconciled us to God, then we are also *delivered in the experience by His life, or in His life.* It is always best to the let the sacred Scriptures explain the scriptures:

> ***For ye are dead, and your life is hid with Christ in God. When Christ, who is our life, shall appear, then shall ye also appear with him in glory.*** **Colossians 3:3-4**

"And not only so, but we also joy in God through our Lord Jesus Christ, by whom we have now received the atonement." - There is more! We can live in *abundant joy* because we are living in union with the Risen Christ. Those who trust in Christ need to be living the victorious life and enjoy our relationship with Jesus every day. The Greek word here for *atonement* is *katallage*, and it simply means reconciliation. Paul reaches the conclusion of an extensive section that began back in **Romans 3:21.** *Reconciliation* to a holy God required the death of Jesus on the cross, and it requires a human response to Him by having faith in His work alone.

ADAM AND CHRIST

> **Romans 5:12 -** ***Wherefore, as by one man sin entered into the world, and death by sin; and so death passed upon all men, for that all have sinned:***

Because the death, burial, and resurrection of *Yeshua* brings justification to the whole human race, Paul now traces our problem with sin back to its source with the fall of *Adam* and does not pick this incomplete thought back up until **Romans 5:18-19.**

The Gentiles could not assume they were without sin since they were not given the Law, nor could the Jews assume they were automatically saved because they were given the Law. The sin problem blankets both Jew and Gentiles and goes back before the Law was even given. Paul reminds the Roman community that *Adam* was a real person, and what happened in **Genesis 3** has a lasting effect to the present day.

While Satan tempted Eve first, *Adam* was still responsible for his actions and represented humanity. **(I Tim. 2:14)** As a result of **Adam's** sin, ⋆*death* has entered into the world and *has been passed upon all men.* The Creator intended for Adam to live forever, but sin changed everything. Before diseases got into the blood stream of humanity, *Adam* still lived to be 930 years of age, thus proving that God wanted man to live eternally. **(Gen. 5:5)** Since *Adam* sinned, all men are subject to *death*, even the smallest ⋆ *baby*. It proves that all of mankind is under the curse of sin.

⋆ *(The real author of death is Satan. The Bible calls the work of evil in the world, "the mystery of iniquity."* **2 Thess. 2:7.** *Why did God allow Satan to tempt Adam? Worship is not true worship if it is forced upon Adam or anyone else. Worshipping God is a free will that God gave to each person. As strange as it may sound, God used Satan to see if Adam would choose to worship Him or choose to listen to the Devil that was cast out of heaven as a result of his own choice.* **(Revelation 12:1-9)** *God did not create evil, evil is simply the absence of good. The Creator God gave man and the angels a choice to worship Him, not a dictatorship to be under obligation.* **Genesis 6:1-4, 2 Peter 2:4, Jude 6)**

⋆ *(This author believes that babies are under the watchful care of a loving Almighty God until they reach the age of accountability for their sins. That age is different for each individual. Read* **Genesis 18:25, 2 Samuel 12:23, Psalm 68:5, Matthew 18:3-5, I Cor. 7:14.** *The Jewish people believe in the blessedness of children because Jacob pronounced a blessing upon his children in his dying breath,* **Gen. 49.** *Children do not go to heaven because they are innocent, but because of a loving, merciful Heavenly Father.)*

While it may sound odd to us in our present day, all mankind actually sinned in *Adam*; all have been made sinners by *Adam's* sin. Some may say that it is not fair to be considered a sinner because of *Adam's* sin; however, we are made righteous by One: the last Adam-*Jesus Christ!*

> **Romans 5:13-14 - *(For until the law sin was in the world: but sin is not imputed when there is no law. Nevertheless death reigned from Adam to Moses, even over them that had not sinned after the similitude of Adam's transgression, who is the figure of him that was to come.***

Sin and death were in the world long before the Law was ever given to Moses. We need to keep in mind that there were Jewish believers within the Christian community of Rome. Paul had to address some of their thoughts and questions concerning *sin and the Law.* The Law was too late to *prevent* sin from coming into the world, and after the Law was given to Moses, it could not *save* anyone from sin. Even though the believers in Rome had not sinned in the same *similitude*, or the same way that Adam sinned, the principle of sin was still at work from Adam. All of the people before the Law were sinners, even those who were Old Testament *saints* who lived *before Moses,* like the ★ *Patriarchs and Matriarchs* of Israel who *all died.*

★ *(Patriarchs, or the Hebrew "avot," are considered to be Abraham, Isaac, Jacob, and Joseph. Matriarchs, or the Hebrew "imahot," are considered to be Sarah, Rebecca, Rachel, and Leah.)*

"who is the figure of him that was to come." **-** Adam is a type - a picture, a representation - of Jesus. Adam *sinned*, but Jesus was *sinless.* What Adam did affected the entire human race *negatively*, and what Jesus did on the cross has affected the entire human race *positively*! Adam is the head of the fallen race derived by sin, while Jesus Christ is the head of the redeemed race being the source of redemption. Only through faith in the finished work of Christ can the *reign of sin* be broken.

> ***And so it is written, The first man Adam was made a living soul; the last Adam (Jesus) was made a quickening spirit.* (I Cor. 15:45)**
>
> ***Forasmuch then as the children are partakers of flesh and blood, he also himself likewise took part of the same; that through death he might destroy him that had the power of death, that is, the devil; And deliver them who through fear of death were all their lifetime subject to bondage.* Hebrews 2:14-15**

When we are born into this world, it is certain we will die physically. The world is really the land of the dying, not the land of the living. It is not a matter of *if* we will die, but *when* we will die. When we look at a cemetery, we are reminded that physical death is coming to all of us if the Lord Jesus should tarry His coming. Paul is giving the believers in Rome and to us today the blessed words that the *reign of life* through Jesus is <u>much more</u> certain than even physical death. *Hallelujah!*

Contrast Between Adam and Christ

> **Romans 5:15-17 - *But not as the offence, so also is the free gift. For if through the offence of one many be dead, much more the grace of God, and the gift***

by grace, which is by one man, Jesus Christ, hath abounded unto many. And not as it was by one that sinned, so is the gift: for the judgment was by one to condemnation, but the free gift is of many offences unto justification. For if by one man's offence death reigned by one; much more they which receive abundance of grace and of the gift of righteousness shall reign in life by one, Jesus Christ.)

The Jewish Paul once again uses the words *"much more"* twice in this passage which is the Hebrew style, *kal-ve'chomer,* showing again the *Hebraisms* behind the Greek text. If the *offence of Adam* brought death into the world, *how much more has Jesus Christ brought righteousness and life into the world* to whosoever will exercise their faith in Him? The word *"many"* is the Greek word, *"polus"* and refers to the countless multitudes of people down through the ages that have died through the sin of Adam.

As a result of Adam's sin, *judgment led to ⋆ condemnation,* but the *free gift* of *God's grace through Christ has brought justification* to all who believe. All of our *offences* were laid upon Jesus on the cross.

⋆ *(This has been a stumbling block to countless people over the centuries. Many believe that if they live a good moral life, that God will not let them go to hell. What Paul is saying is that we are under condemnation not because of our specific sins of commission or omission, but because sin and death reign over us because of Adam. The best person cannot enter into a perfect heaven without the righteousness of Christ. The condemnation rate is 100 percent until a person receives Jesus into his life.)*

> **Romans 5:18 -** ***Therefore as by the offence of one*** *(Adam)* ***judgment came upon * all men to condemnation; even so by the righteousness of one*** *(Jesus)* ***the free gift came upon * all men unto justification of life.***

While this may start sounding redundant, it is very important for us to establish these important truths into our lives. We are either identified in *one Adam* or identified in *one Jesus.* We will either die <u>in</u> our sins **(John 8:24)** or die <u>in</u> the righteousness of Christ. Every human is born into this world under the *judgment of Adam,* but we can be *born again* into the *eternal life of Jesus Christ.* Because of His great love of mankind, it is a *free gift*! It is the nature of a *gift* that it <u>must be received</u>.

★ *(Because of the Greek and English wording here, the little word "all" in this verse has caused much debate over the centuries, even among the so-called scholars of the Bible. There is only one Greek word for "all" and that is "pas," which does somewhat correlate with the Hebrew word, "kowl," but the <u>Hebrew thought</u> goes farther. If we go back to the deeper Hebrew mindset of Paul, we find that the word "all" can mean "everyone, or it can mean whosoever." So the first "all" is referring to <u>everyone</u> is under condemnation, while the second "all" is referring <u>to only those who receive the free gift of Christ</u> for justification of life. The doctrine of Universalism is taught in some religious circles where every human being will be saved in the end. This author believes that the Holy Bible <u>does not</u> teach Universalism! Paul is showing the contrast between "all" being guilty of sin and the free gift belonging to "all" or "whosoever" will receive Christ.)*

★ Adam - judgment & condemnation

★ Jesus - free gift & justification

Romans 5:19 - ***For as by one man's disobedience ★ many were made sinners, so by the obedience of one shall ★ many be made righteous.***

Adam's disobedience made *everyone* a sinner, and Jesus' obedience makes *many* righteous. We see again the results of TWO MEN - Adam and Jesus. The sinless Son of God came to deliver us from something that another man caused. If someone wants to stand on his own and he does not like the rules, it really is not up to us. God made the rules!

Paul is repeating what he has previously stated by a mere rephrasing. Notice that instead of Adam's offence here, it is Adam's *disobedience.* The righteous work of Christ is called *obedience.*

★ *(We have again the word "many" that has caused some to be confused. The Greek word is "polus" coming from "hoi polloi" where Paul uses it in the first part of the verse to refer to the totality of Adam's disobedience. The second time the word "many" refers to those who shall be constituted righteous through personal faith in Christ.)*

Law and Grace

Romans 5:20-21 - ***Moreover the law entered, that the offence might abound. But where sin abounded, grace did much more abound: That as sin hath reigned unto***

> ***death, even so might grace reign through righteousness unto eternal life by Jesus Christ our Lord.***

The Law shows that the evil inclination of man desires what is prohibited. The Law does not make us sinners. Adam caused the sin to come into the world. The Law's purpose is to help us see our sins clearer and greater. The Law draws clear lines that we sinful humans want to cross. Using the Hebrew style *much more* again, the Law causes sin *to abound,* the grace of God *much more abounds under Jesus.* We deserve the wrath of God, but through the offering of Christ on the cross, we can see that God's grace is much greater than our sins. Wow! It is hard for a sinner to out-sin God's grace!

When we think of sin, it brings the thought of *death*, but when we think of *grace*, we think of *the righteousness of Jesus Christ our Lord that brings eternal life.* Paul has something more in mind here. When we receive the grace of God and are imputed the righteousness of Christ our Lord, we start to let *grace reign* in our daily lives. We become united with God's grace in all that we say and do. Grace does not give anyone a license to sin.

> ***For the grace of God that bringeth salvation hath appeared to all men, Teaching us that, denying ungodliness and worldly lusts, we should live soberly, righteously, and godly, in this present world;* Titus 2:11-12**

This thought leads Paul into the next chapter where he discusses living the Christian life, with Jesus being the Lord of our lives.

CHAPTER SIX

Freedom From Habitual Sins

Romans 6:1-2 - ***What shall we say then? Shall we continue in sin, that grace may abound? God forbid. How shall we, that are dead to sin, live any longer therein?***

Paul uses two Hebrew styles of teaching here. The first is *libertinism* where he takes up the argument from the end of the last chapter **(Romans 5:20)** where he suggests that people may engage in sin in order to give God's grace an opportunity to increase or *abound.* In Jewish style, Paul raises this erroneous conclusion in order to immediately refute it. The second Hebrew style is *chalilah* where he says *"God forbid"* or *"be far from it."* **(Romans 3:6)**

If God loves the sinner and we are saved by grace, then why not sin more and receive more grace? While it is ludicrous, there have been ⋆ religious leaders from various circles over the centuries who have taught that through repeated circumstances of sin one receives the most forgiveness.

⋆ *(While the doctrine of eternal security of the believer is clearly taught in the sacred scriptures in many places such as* **John 10:28-29,**

I John 5:13, *much damage has been done to God's kingdom by not focusing more on holy living. Our motivation to live a godly life is not moralism or trying to be better, but living a godly life because of what Jesus has done for us.)*

> **Romans 6:3-4 -** ***Know ye not, that so many of us as were baptized into Jesus Christ were baptized into his death? Therefore we are buried with him by baptism into death: that like as Christ was raised up from the dead by the glory of the Father, even so we also should walk in newness of life.***

The misunderstanding of this passage has caused much division in the body of Christ over the centuries, and some churches even base their doctrine of *water baptismal regeneration* upon this passage. It is sad when people get lost in a symbol and lose sight of the Savior! There is no evidence in the New Testament that *water baptism* changes anyone's life at the moment they are *covered* in water. So we will strive to help the reader better understand Paul's intent.

The ancient, Jewish idea behind *water baptism* was to be *immersed* in water in order to be identified with purification, repentance *(John the Baptist)* or someone *(Jesus the Messiah).* When someone is *immersed* in water, he is *covered* with water. When we are *immersed* in the Holy Spirit, we are *covered* with the Holy Spirit. **(Matt.3:1, Acts 1:5)** When we are *baptized or immersed* in suffering, we are *covered* with suffering like Jesus. **(Mark 10:39)** In this passage Paul is referring to our spiritual union with Christ, or our being *covered* with Christ, which is brought about when we are *immersed* by the Holy Spirit.

> ***For by one Spirit are we all baptized into one body, whether we be Jews or Gentiles, whether we be bond or free; and have been all made to drink into one Spirit.*** **I Corinthians 12:13**

Water baptism is the outward sign that we have been identified with the death, burial, and resurrection of Jesus Christ and have *already* been born again of the Holy Spirit.

> ***For as many of you as have been baptized into Christ have put on Christ.*** **Galatians 3:27**

When we compare the scriptures of **Romans 6, I Cor. 12, and Galatians 3,** it is clear that the only viable conclusion to this passage is the *baptism of the Holy Spirit.* The Holy Spirit *baptism* or *immersion* is what affects our union with Jesus Christ and the way we live our daily lives. This is why countless people have been *water baptized* and never truly experienced a changed life. Every person who has been saved by God's grace should be *water baptized;* not in order to be saved, but to show unashamedly that we are *already* saved and want to be *identified* with Christ.

Notice the words *"death"* and *"dead"* in **Romans 6:1-2.** As Christ *died*, was buried, and rose again, we have *died* to the old person we were before we met Christ. We cannot die and rise again with Christ without the experience of a change in our lives. The believer in Christ has a real *union* with His death and resurrection.

"That like as Christ was raised up from the dead by the glory of the Father, even so we also should walk in newness of life." - This implies that the Christian can *walk in the newness of life* by the same glory. The Christian's life is not just repeating a prayer, attending Bible study, keeping an ordinance, or turning over a new leaf. It is connected to the *dynamic power* that raised Jesus from the dead. This is how we can overcome the sinfulness of the flesh, as Paul will later point out in **Romans 8.** This is why we must never demean salvation to just being religious mechanics. It is a supernatural miracle to be born again! We have the power within us to live the life that Christ has ordained us to live. People who have been regenerated by the Holy Spirit have been called to *walk in a newness of life* that reflects God's kingdom.

> **Romans 6:5-10 - *For if we have been planted together in the likeness of his death, we shall be also in the likeness of his resurrection: Knowing this, that our old man is crucified with him, that the body of sin might be destroyed, that henceforth we should not serve sin. For he that is dead is freed from sin. Now if we be dead with Christ, we believe that we shall also live with him: Knowing that Christ being raised from the dead dieth no more; death hath no more dominion over him. For in that he died, he died unto sin once: but in that he liveth, he liveth unto God.***

When we look at this section as a whole, it is evident that Paul is not talking about our *future resurrection,* but discussing our walk in *the newness of life.* The Greek word *planted* is *sumphutos,* and it means *"united."* We could never be *co-crucified* with Christ physically, so Paul changes the wording here to refer to our *old sinful man* that has been *planted*, or *united* with the death of Christ. We have been saved and have the power not to *serve* sin. Christians cannot live the life that Jesus has called us to live in the power of the flesh. The struggle between the flesh and the Spirit goes on within the life of every believer. We stumble and sin from time to time, but we do not *habitually sin* because of the indwelling power of the Holy Spirit convicting us when we sin. Our inner lives have been *healed or joined* together with the work of Jesus. There is a strong hidden connection here to what the prophet Isaiah wrote seven centuries before. When prophesying about the death of Israel's Messiah in **Isaiah 53,** the word *"stripes"* is the Hebrew word "chaburah" and it means "to join." We have been joined with the suffering of Christ and therefore are spiritually healed. Wow!

> ***But he was wounded for our transgressions, he was bruised for our iniquities: the chastisement of our peace was upon him; and with his stripes (Hebrew chaburah) we are healed.*** **Isaiah 53:5**

Paul would later write these words:

> ***I am crucified with Christ: nevertheless I live; yet not I, but Christ liveth in me: and the life which I now live in the flesh I live by the faith of the Son of God, who loved me, and gave himself for me.*** **Galatians 2:20**

"Now if we be dead with Christ, we believe that we shall also live with him:" - Sometimes we are guilty of focusing too much on the cross of Christ without focusing on what follows. There is nothing spiritual about bowing before a crucifix or wearing one around our necks. We not only will *live with Christ* one day in heaven, but we can *live with Him* each day in the power of the resurrection. Note what Paul wrote from a prison cell:

> ***That I may know him, and the power of his resurrection, and the fellowship of his sufferings, being made conformable unto his death; If by any means I might attain unto the resurrection of the dead.*** **Philippians 3:10-11**

Paul lived his life in striving to know more about the power of Christ's resurrection. We must reckon the *old man* within us as dead and not allow the emotions, passions, and evil desires of the flesh to control us:

> ***That ye put off concerning the former conversation the old man, which is corrupt according to the deceitful lusts.*** **Ephesians 4:22**

"Knowing that Christ being raised from the dead dieth no more; death hath no more dominion over him. For in that he died, he died unto sin once: but in that he liveth, he liveth unto God" **-** The life that we now live in Christ is part of *His Eternal Life*! Once we were *joined* to the old slavery of sin, but now we *live* as free unto righteousness. There was a time when sin and death ruled over us as a tyrant, but now we live in the victory of the Risen Christ! Hallelujah! Jesus only died *once*, and He only arose from the grave *once*. We are born into this world in the flesh one time, and we can be born of the Spirit only one time. Just as Jesus cannot return to the grave, we cannot be *saved-lost-resaved*. Eternal Life is a gift from God and while we may never reach our potential in what we should be for Jesus in this life, once we are saved we are *eternally saved*! As death has no power over Jesus, He conquered death; the old life we used to live has no power over us anymore. Since Jesus took our sins to the cross, *He now lives forevermore.* Sin does not have power over us anymore, and we can *live unto God* because He has written His laws on our *hearts* and given us peace, joy, and purpose. Again, Paul is writing to the Roman community of believers with the argument of how they are *saved by grace* but are *not free* to live a life of sin. This is a feature of the New Covenant that was prophesied in the Old Testament where we are given *new hearts:*

> ***A new heart also will I give you, and a new spirit will I put within you: and I will take away the stony heart out of your flesh, and I will give you an heart of flesh. And I will put my spirit within you, and cause you to walk in my statutes, and ye shall keep my judgments, and do them.*** **Ezekiel 36:26-27**

> **Romans 6:11-12 -** ***Likewise reckon ye also yourselves to be dead indeed unto sin, but alive unto God through Jesus Christ our Lord. Let not sin therefore reign in your mortal body, that ye should obey it in the lusts thereof.***

We have to be united with Christ in His death and resurrection if we are going to walk in the newness of life. We being human, we also have to *reckon ourselves dead unto sin.* The Greek word for *reckon* is *logizomai*, and it is the very same word that Paul used for *imputed* in **Romans 4.** Thus the man or woman whom God *imputes* righteousness to should also *impute or reckon* himself or herself *dead to sin and alive unto God through Jesus Christ our Lord.* We are declared righteous by faith, and we live by faith!

With this in view, we need to orient our behavior in the light of this truth. Paul is telling the believers in Rome that in their unregenerate past days they allowed sin to *reign in their mortal bodies and they obeyed it with its lusts.* Now they are no longer to give in to those sinful desires. Only a person who has been set free from sin can be told, *"do not let sin reign in your mortal body."* Our desires have been changed to honor God and to please Him. Many Christians are not living in this freedom because of lack of faith, ignorance, or they are relying on the power of the flesh to live the Christian life.

> **Romans 6:13-14 - *Neither yield ye your members as instruments of unrighteousness unto sin: but yield yourselves unto God, as those that are alive from the dead, and your members as instruments of righteousness unto God. For sin shall not have dominion over you: for ye are not under the law, but under grace.***

Paul mentions that the Roman community *does* not *yield their members as instruments of unrighteousness unto sin.* He is referring to all parts of the body, such as the ears, lips, eyes, hands, and mind. The Greek word for *yield* is *paristemi*, and it means *"to put at someone's disposal."* A Christian is to place his body at God's disposal for His purpose. Our attitudes and actions should be joined together. Giving lip service to God will not help; it is only a high form of hypocrisy. Once a caterpillar has been made a butterfly, the butterfly has no business crawling around on trees and leaves anymore. It is free to fly and to show forth in its new beauty for what God has made it to be.

The Greek word for *members* is *melos* and was used in Bible times to refer to the instruments of war or the working parts of a ship. The *members* of our body can be used as weapons ★ against evil, or they be used in the service of sin.

★ *(David used his body to defeat Goliath in* **I Samuel 17,** *and then he yielded his body to commit sin with Bathsheba in* **2 Samuel 11.** *When using the term "members," Paul may have been referring to the open sexual sins that were so prevalent in the Roman world. The believers in Rome were surrounded by immorality on a scale that our minds cannot even comprehend; from adultery, to homosexuality, and even to sexual relations with animals (bestiality). Paul was teaching the young believers in Jesus the vast contrast between living a pagan, sexual lifestyle to living a Christian sexual lifestyle and honoring God with their bodies. The world we are living in today is fast becoming a Christ-less society with sexual sins much like it was in Rome.)*

In a similar manner the priests in the Old Testament consecrated their bodies to God. Notice how they applied the sacrificial blood:

> ***Then shalt thou kill the ram, and take of his blood, and put it upon the tip of the right ear of Aaron, and upon the tip of the right ear of his sons, and upon the thumb of their right hand, and upon the great toe of their right foot, and sprinkle the blood upon the altar round about.*** **Exodus 29:20**

"For sin shall not have dominion over you: for ye are not under the law, but under grace." - This does not mean that sin is not present with the Christian, nor does it mean that a Christian cannot and does not sin. **(I John 1:8-10)** Because we have been given a righteous standing before God through faith in the finished work of Christ alone, the Holy Spirit comes to live inside of us and gives us freedom! Sin *does not have dominion over us* because we are not living under a legalistic system or trying to keep the Law, but we are now under God's amazing *grace*! As stated earlier, the Law clearly defined God's holy standards, but the Law cannot give us the freedom from sin that *grace* provides. Paul is still giving an answer to the question in **Romans 6:1; *"What shall we say then? Shall we continue in sin, that grace may abound?"*** The changes in our lives may not come all at once, but the changes are real and God's Holy Spirit will not let one of His children sin without bringing conviction. Notice these verses:

> ***Whosoever abideth in him sinneth not: whosoever sinneth hath not seen him, neither known him.*** *(Does not habitually sin.)* ***I John 3:6***
>
> ***Whosoever is born of God doth not commit sin; for his seed remaineth in him: and he cannot sin, because he is born of God.*** *(A Christian does not practice sin because the Holy Spirit within us cannot sin.)* **I John 3:9**
>
> **Romans 6:15-16** - ***What then? shall we * sin, because we are not under the law, but under grace? God forbid. Know ye not, that to whom ye yield yourselves servants to obey, his servants ye are to***

whom ye obey; whether of sin unto death, or of obedience unto righteousness?

Again, Paul is saying that grace does not give a believer the license to sin. Paul uses the Hebrew idiom of *chalilah* again, *"God forbid."* Why would a child of God even consider getting away with sin? We are supposed to be honoring God in all that we do and remember that as followers of Christ, we are to represent God's kingdom. Who will we serve? Will we be servants of evil or servants of righteousness? If we *disobey* and turn our lives over to be servants of evil, then it will lead to *death*, but if we turn our lives over to be servants of *obedience*, then it leads to *righteousness.*

* *(The Greek word for sin here is hamartano and it is different from the word for sin in* **Romans 6:1** *where it speaks of habitual sins. The sin in* **Romans 6:15** *means missing the mark, or making a mistake. Many Christians think that because we are saved by God's grace, then it is okay to dibble dabble in sin. This can lead to a premature physical death in the life of a Christian.* **I Corinthians 3:15-16, 5:5)**

Romans 6:17-18 - ***But God be thanked, that ye were the servants of sin, but ye have obeyed from the heart that form of doctrine which was delivered you. Being then made free from sin, ye became the servants of righteousness.***

Paul is grateful to God that the believers in Rome were no longer *slaves to sin,* as they had *sincerely obeyed from their heart and responded to the form of doctrine they had received.* They submitted themselves without reservation to the doctrine they were taught. It is interesting that the Greek word for *form* is *tupos*, and it means *"stamped, or a pattern."* In simple words, Paul's *form of doctrine* was the same pattern that God had given him. The other apostles had taught this *form of doctrine* when they were traveling, and Paul was not giving the Roman believers some new form of doctrine. This idea also carries with it that as believers in Christ the Lord, we are being molded into the impression of His likeness. Believers in Christ have a new boss over their lives and have been *made free from sin, and become servants of righteousness.*

> **Romans 6:19 - *I speak after the manner of men because of the infirmity of your flesh: for as ye have yielded your members servants to uncleanness and to iniquity unto iniquity; even so now yield your members servants to righteousness unto holiness.***

Although he did not like using the term slavery as an illustration, Paul is using terminology due to the *weakness of the flesh.* They, like Paul and all of us, are human beings who need wording we can understand and apply the truths to our lives. In the past they had been ★ *slaves to a vicious cycle of uncleanness that led to nothing but a life of iniquity that produced nothing else;* only vanity and empty living. The energy and time they had once used to serve wickedness, they needed to use now for holy living. Their lives can now be a shining light to each other and to those around them and count for something in eternity.

★ *(In the Roman world the people were very familiar with the concept of someone who was permanently attached to a pagan temple as a servant of the god who was worshipped there. Paul is showing them that they not only have been set free from a world that is going to perish, but they have been placed in service of the one true God Almighty. Like trees that grow year after year, the longer they are rooted in Christ, the harder it will be for Satan to snatch them back again.)*

> **Romans 6:20-21 - *For when ye were the servants of sin, ye were free from righteousness. What fruit had ye then in those things whereof ye are now ashamed? for the end of those things is death.***

As Paul continues to expand his analogy between the old servitude and the new one, the believers in Jesus needed to remember when they were lost in sin, they were producing no *spiritual fruit.* God reminds us from time to time about our past, not to condemn us, but to show us that the things we used to serve we are now ashamed of.

"for the end of those things is death." **-** The *fruit of sin is death*! Not only had their previous lives been an *experience of death* while on earth, it would lead to a life of *eternal death.* If someone has not been born again, he is considered to be *dead in trespasses and sins.* **(Ephesians 2:1)**

> **Romans 6:22-23 - *But now being made free from sin, and become servants to God, ye have your fruit unto holiness, and the end everlasting life. For the wages of sin is death; but the gift of God is eternal life through Jesus Christ our Lord.***

Note the contrast when Paul uses the words *fruit unto holiness, and the end everlasting life!* All who belong to Christ need to see the vast difference between the *fruits of sin unto death and the fruits of holiness unto life.* Not only does Jesus save us and place us in His kingdom, He gives our life purpose and meaning. We are bringing forth spiritual fruit! Hallelujah!

"For the wages of sin is death; but the gift of God is eternal life through Jesus Christ our Lord" - How much deeper this familiar verse is when we study it as the end of this powerful *pericope* that Paul has been teaching in this chapter. Most of the time this verse is just quoted out of context, and we do not have a chance to grasp the entire meaning. Death is the compensation that *we earn* when we live a life of sin; it is our *wages.* And yes, the reason everyone has to die physically is because sin came into the world through Adam. *But eternal life is not something that we earn or deserve; it is a gift from God through Jesus Christ our Lord,* the last Adam! When we embrace Christ, we are receiving a *gift.* When we produce a life of holiness and fruitful living, we are living out this *gift.*

The closing words of this chapter serve as a closing to this unit by using the powerful words *Christo Iesou to Kyrio, Christ Jesus the Lord.* Christ or Messiah is Jesus the Lord! Our union with Jesus, who died and rose again, is what gives us the *gift* of the newness of life which begins by enjoying His *eternal life* here and now!

CHAPTER SEVEN

Relationship to the Law Has Ended

> **Romans 7:1-4** - ***Know ye not, brethren, (for I speak to them that know the law,) how that the law hath dominion over a man as long as he liveth? For the woman which hath an husband is bound by the law to her husband so long as he liveth; but if the husband be dead, she is loosed from the law of her husband. So then if, while her husband liveth, she be married to another man, she shall be called an adulteress: but if her husband be dead, she is free from that law; so that she is no adulteress, though she be married to another man. Wherefore, my brethren, ye also are become dead to the law by the body of Christ; that ye should be married to another, even to him who is raised from the dead, that we should bring forth fruit unto God.***

What about the Jewish believers *(brethren)* in Rome who were confused about trying to keep the Law as many of the rabbis had said? What about the Gentile believers in Christ who were being told by some Jews that they needed to still keep the Law? Paul uses the analogy of a Jewish woman who is married under Jewish law. While he does not mention both reasons here, there were only two ways that a Jewish woman could remarry once she was married; 1. *If there had been grounds for a divorce* **(Deut. 24:1-2)** 2. *Or the death of the husband which Paul illustrates here.* The point that Paul is making is not about a Jewish marriage per say, it is about being dead to the Law. The basic principle is that the Law is only applicable to people who are alive. Although the Law has timeless principles of righteous living, the Jewish believer in Christ has been freed from the Mosaic Law. They were dead to the Law so they could ★ *marry* Christ. If the Jewish believers in Christ kept trying to be married to the Law, they were committing spiritual adultery. They had been set free not to live unto themselves, but free to bear fruit for Jesus who was raised from the dead.

★ *(Both Jew and Gentile believers make up the Bride of Christ.* **(Ephesians 5:25)** *Over 15 verses in the New Testament refer to Jesus as the Bridegroom, and he gave numerous parables and teachings with the background of a Jewish wedding. Unbelieving Israel had committed spiritual adultery by claiming to know the Law and then rejecting its Messiah.)*

Our union with Jesus Christ has linked us to the experience of His own body in which He bore the penalty that the Law required for sin. Why would Jesus die that horrible death on the tree if He wanted His children to live back under the Law? Notice Paul's words to the Galatians:

> ***Christ hath redeemed us from the curse of the law, being made a curse for us: for it is written, Cursed is every one that hangeth on a tree:*** **Galatians 3:13**

Romans 7:5 - ***For when we were in the flesh, the motions of sins, which were by the law, did work in our members to bring forth fruit unto death.***

In describing this pre-conversional experience, Paul now switches from the singular *"ye"* to the plural *"we"* to include himself. Paul wanted the Jewish believers in Rome to know his own experiences with the Law. Because of the evil inclinations of sinful humans, the Law awakened the forbidden sins of the flesh. It is comparable to people seeing a sign telling them not to do something their evil impulse will want them to do. Paul is saying that when *we were in the flesh,* the Law brought out the Greek *pathema; motion, suffering, or passions of sins.* Even though the Law was good, sinful man trying to keep the Law results in *fruits unto death.* We can only bear spiritual fruit when we are free from the Law.

Romans 7:6 - ***But now we are delivered from the law, that being dead wherein we were held; that we should serve in newness of spirit, and not in the oldness of the letter.***

Even though this all may sound repetitious to us living almost 2,000 years later, Paul is having to deal with *delivering* people, some his own brethren Jews, from thinking that the Law could save them. He helped them to let go of many of their Jewish traditions and customs to follow Christ. Sometimes Christians today are still in bondage to a denomination, or some rule they were raised to believe, or some pet doctrine they have been taught, and they need to be *delivered.*

Paul includes himself in saying that *we are delivered from the Law* as a means of justification or of sanctification. They had been *held back* by their former relationship to the Law. The same God who wrote the Law on tablets of stone for Moses and the children of Israel had come in the flesh of Jesus of Nazareth to die for their sins, and had written His Law on their hearts. They were to serve Him with a greater fervor and *newness of spirit* more than they served in the *letter of the Law.* They were now under the *New Covenant.* Notice these words that Paul wrote to the church in Corinth:

> ***But their minds were blinded: for until this day remaineth the same vail untaken away in the reading of the old testament; which vail is done away in Christ. 2 Corinthians 3:14***

God's Perfect Law and Sinful Man

> **Romans 7:7 - *What shall we say then? Is the law sin? God forbid. Nay, I had not known sin, but by the law: for I had not known lust, except the law had said, Thou shalt not covet.***

Paul's negative assessment of the Law's impact on sin might lead to the question, *"Is the law sin?"* Once again Paul uses the Hebrew idiom *chalilah* to say *God forbid.* It is unthinkable for them to imagine that God's Law was sinful. The perfect Law served a purpose in actually exposing sin like an x-ray machine. A good example is the sin of *lust.* How would a person know that it was wrong unless God's Law told them

"Thou shalt not covet?" **(Exodus 20:17)** The problem is not God's Law, the problem is man's sin.

> **Romans 7:8 - *But sin, taking occasion by the commandment, wrought in me all manner of concupiscence. For without the law sin was dead.***

Paul is using himself as an example here. When he read the commandment about not coveting his neighbor's wife, all manner of *concupiscence,* or the Greek *epithumia, evil, passionate longings* arose in his heart. Sin took advantage of Paul by drawing forth the sinful desires that were a part of his nature. *Sin is not recognized and is dead* apart from the prohibition of the Law. This is how great the sin of evil is within every human being. Sin can take something good and holy like the Law and twist it into promoting evil. Sin can warp love into lust, or an honest desire to work for a living into greed and love of money.

> **Romans 7:9 - *For I was alive without the law once: but when the commandment came, sin revived, and I died.***

Paul is still giving parts of his own biography. He had considered himself *alive once without the Law.* He even told the Sanhedrin that he lived with a *good conscience* in **Acts 23:1.** When Paul was confronted with the Law, he saw how sinful he was, and ⋆ *he died.*

⋆ *(The word "once" refers to an unspecified time in Paul's life. Perhaps Paul "died to sin" on the Damascus Road in* **Acts 9:9,** *or perhaps in Arabia in* **Galatians 1:17.** *Between the phases of him considering himself "once alive" and "dying to sin," there was a phase* *of Paul's life when he also considered himself blameless and zealous toward the Law.* **Philippians 3:5-6***)*

> **Romans 7:10-12** - ***And the commandment, which was ordained to life, I found to be unto death. For sin, taking occasion by the commandment, deceived me, and by it slew me. Wherefore the law is holy, and the commandment holy, and just, and good.***

It was not the Law that deceived Paul; it was the sin. Sin uses God's *commandments* as a means of deception. God's intention of the Law was to have a positive effect, not a negative effect. The *commandments* written in the Law were to keep man from sinning that would lead to death. As was the case with Eve in the *Garden of Eden,* **(Genesis 3:1-5)** Satan tells us that God is withholding something good from us and wants to deprive us of something. A loving God warns us to stay away from sin that will lead to our own destruction. The experience of Paul being *killed by the Law* in no way diminishes the sanctity of the Law. The character of God's Law is ⋆ *holy, and just, and good.* Even though Paul experienced a "fall" because of his own sins, the Law still served its true purpose in exposing his sin.

⋆ *(If a ship is launched out at sea, then sinks with good vessels on board, the entire ship goes down with the vessels; but not so with the Law. Just because man sins and breaks the Law, which results in death, man does not cause the Law to perish; it remains holy and glorious.)*

> **Romans 7:13-14** - ***Was then that which is good made death unto me? God forbid. But sin, that it might appear sin, working death in me by that***

which is good; that sin by the commandment might become exceeding sinful. For we know that the law is spiritual: but I am carnal, sold under sin.

If sin can use something as good as the Law to its advantage in promoting evil, it shows how evil sin really is. One of the most deplorable things about sin is that it wants to conceal the consequences of the sin. The reason why people do not like to read the Law is because it draws out all kinds of sins and corruption out of us. But again, it is not the Law that is bad; it is the *sin*. Sin is *exceedingly sinful* because it is in contrast to God's perfection, and in defiance produces ⋆ death.

⋆ *(Again, Paul is having to deal with the issue of Jewish believers in Christ who are wrestling with the question of still trying to keep the Law of Moses. We do not need to spend too much time talking about the Law and the results of us failing to keep it without keeping in mind that this is the reason why Jesus lived a perfect life under the Law. He was the embodiment of the Law and then willingly died in our place on the cross so we could be saved.)*

Paul is saying that the Law is not only good, but it is *spiritual*. The Law is a reflection of the *spiritual* nature of God and is not *carnal* as Paul is. While the Apostle Paul was certainly one of the greatest Christians who ever lived, he was still *carnal*, or the Greek *sarkinos*, which means *characterized by the flesh,* as the other Christians that he was writing to. He was not placing himself above everyone else as a better individual. Paul recognizes that the *spiritual* Law cannot help a *carnal* man, and he considers himself *sold under sin*. Even Paul sees that sin has ⋆ dominion over him in the flesh, and his only plea is guilty!

★ *(The wise man knows that he is carnal and is displeased with himself while praising the Law of God. The foolish man is someone who thinks he is spiritual and ends up in a very dangerous position called self-righteousness.)*

Paul's Struggle Within His Own Strength

> **Romans 7:15-19 - *For that which I do I allow not: for what I would, that do I not; but what I hate, that do I. If then I do that which I would not, I consent unto the law that it is good. Now then it is no more I that do it, but sin that dwelleth in me. For I know that in me (that is, in my flesh,) dwelleth no good thing: for to will is present with me; but how to perform that which is good I find not. For the good that I would I do not: but the evil which I would not, that I do.***

One of the key words in this passage is the word "would," or the Greek *thelo*, which means *"wish."* Living the Christian life is far more than just *wishing* to live it. Paul realizes that the problem is not his lack of desire of wanting to do good. The problem is not his lack of knowledge; the problem is his *lack of power.* The Law does not give anyone the power to overcome evil inclinations. Even though Paul was a new man in Christ, he still struggled within his own strength. There are two natures at work when a Christian starts trying to live the kingdom life. The inward person that Christ has created does not want to sin, but the outward man still wants to sin. We need to remember that it is not just the sins of the flesh, but also the ★ sins of the spirit that we sometimes forget. In these verses we see a strange paradox of Paul owning up to his sin and yet disowning it. He was a strong follower of Christ the Lord and had been called to be an Apostle to the Gentiles. And yet, he realized that in *his flesh dwelleth no good thing!*

★ *(People see the outward deeds but God sees the heart. What may appear to be a big success to us may not even register in God's records. What about motives? What about pride? Try to imagine how Paul was given such great revelations and how God used a thorn in the flesh to keep him humble before Him.* **2 Corinthians 12:7-9** *This is why we need to* *be followers of Jesus Christ* *and not followers of Paul or any other Christian. There are many ministers who are so Paulinistic that they try to copy what Paul said and did. Jesus was sinless and Paul said that in his flesh dwelleth no good thing.)*

> **Romans 7:20-23 -** ***Now if I do that I would not, it is no more I that do it, but sin that dwelleth in me. I find then a law, that, when I would do good, evil is present with me. For I delight in the law of God after the inward man: But I see another law in my members, warring against the law of my mind, and bringing me into captivity to the law of sin which is in my members.***

Paul does not share the illusion that some Christians have after they have been regenerated, then obedience to God's Law is both simple and easy. Although the Spirit within us is glorious and life giving, the physical body remains completely dead to God's will. The sinful flesh always desires the opposite of what the Spirit desires. Paul wanted to live as God had called him to live in Christ, but there was still this principle of *Two*

Ways- Flesh or Spirit- Satan or Jesus! This is why it is so important for all of us not to have any confidence in the flesh. *Moralism-Religion-Creeds-Theology-Church-Knowledge* can all be just a work of the flesh. Sin always wins against the weakness of the flesh.

VICTORY IN JESUS CHRIST

> **Romans 7:24-25 - *O wretched man that I am! who shall deliver me from the body of this death? I thank God through Jesus Christ our Lord. So then with the mind I myself serve the law of God; but with the flesh the law of sin.***

The Greek word for *wretched* is *talaiporos*, and it means *"miserable and afflicted."* Trying to serve God in the power of the flesh wears Paul completely out. He wants the Jewish believers in Rome to know that trying to live the Christian life within the power of the flesh will make them *miserable.* Paul is praying that they will see this and not be like the Pharisees of old and deny their sinfulness, but acknowledge it and start following Christ in their daily lives. It all goes beyond a desire to just do better; we must become *wretched* like Paul and cry out to God for deliverance!

"who shall deliver me from the * body of this death?" **-** Every day we live as a Christian, we have to drag this physical body around that is always pulling us down. This is why there are so few Christians living a life of victory because they do not understand how to be controlled by the Holy Spirit.

* *(In the ancient world many times a tyrant who wanted to really punish someone would tie his live body up to a dead body and place them back to back. While this seems extreme, the point should paint*

the morbid picture of how being a Christian and trying to live a life powered by the flesh really is.)

"I thank God through Jesus Christ our Lord" - Paul has referred to himself some 40 times in this chapter, and now he states the only answer to his rescue - ***Jesus Christ our Lord!*** Jesus is standing between Paul and God and gives him the victory. *Jesus Christ* was God in the flesh that came to earth from heaven to live a life as the perfect ⋆*Man* to be our Lord and Master. He did not come to this earth just to give us better rules to live by, but to give us the victory! As we surrender our lives to Jesus, we can have victory over sin, hate, and all manner of evil in our lives. We do not need a teacher, a motivational speaker, or a doctor; we need a Savior! The Law ⋆⋆ shows us that we need the man Jesus Christ! When we see Jesus our Lord in heaven, He will still be in the form of a *Man*!

⋆ *(For there is one God, and one mediator between God and men, the man Christ Jesus.)* I Timothy 2:5

> ***And I turned to see the voice that spake with me. And being turned, I saw seven golden candlesticks; And in the midst of the seven candlesticks one like unto the <u>Son of man</u>, clothed with a garment down to the foot, and girt about the paps with a golden girdle.***
> **Revelation 1:12-13**

⋆⋆ *(Wherefore the law was our schoolmaster to bring us unto Christ, that we might be justified by faith.)* Galatians 3:24

"So then with the mind I myself (Greek *autos ego*) ***serve the law of God; but with the flesh the law of sin"*** - This is a powerful little statement that Paul is making. He emphatically says that the *"true I"* serve *the law of God.* That is the new man that Christ has made him to be. Notice the contrast in the second phrase where he says it with less emphasis and separates his flesh from the *"true I,"* that *the flesh serves the law of sin.*

CHAPTER EIGHT

NEW LIFE IN THE HOLY SPIRIT

Romans 8:1 - *There is therefore now no condemnation to them which are in Christ Jesus, who walk not after the flesh, but after the Spirit.*

The Greek word for *condemnation* here is *katakrima*, and it means *"penalty or judgment."* We would be wise to remember that there were no chapters in the original text, and Paul makes this statement immediately after he talks about how sinful he is in the flesh, and after writing so many verses about the confusion and conflict of the Law. The key here is that if we are *in Christ Jesus, there is no condemnation.* Since God the Father accepted what Jesus did on the cross, neither does He *condemn* those who are *in Jesus.* They cannot be *condemned*! This chapter begins with no *condemnation*, in between there is no *defeat*, and at the end of the chapter there is no *separation.* There is a real, yet mystical, union between Christ and His people. It has to be more than just mental accentuation to Jesus Christ; the person has to be *in Christ:*

> ***Then Jesus said unto them, Verily, verily, I say unto you, Except ye eat the flesh of the Son of man, and drink his blood, ye have no life in you. Whoso eateth my flesh, and drinketh my blood, hath eternal life; and I will raise him up at the last day. For my flesh is meat indeed, and my blood is drink indeed. He that eateth my flesh, and drinketh my blood, dwelleth in me, and I in him.*** **John 6:53-56**

Just like the people who ate the bread and the fish when Jesus fed the multitude in **John 6:1-14,** we must *internalize* Jesus. Some people may say things like, *"I'm trying to do better"* or *"I'm a member of a church."* The difference is having Jesus Christ living within us; that is how we live the life that Paul is referring to. If a person is Christian in name only, he is still under the judgment of the Lord.

"who walk not after the flesh, but after the Spirit" **-** This phrase is repeated in **verse 4.** The second step is that we must *walk*, or *peripateo, not after the flesh, but after the Spirit.* In the Hebrew thought it means *how we conduct our lives.* There is no judgment or condemnation upon us when we are *in Christ and walking after the Spirit!* We are still confronted by the flesh, but the Spirit is more powerful than the flesh!

> **Romans 8:2-4** - ***For the law of the Spirit of life in Christ Jesus hath made me free from the law of sin and death. For what the law could not do, in that it was weak through the flesh, God sending his own Son in the likeness of sinful flesh, and for sin, condemned sin in the flesh: That the righteousness of the law might be fulfilled in us, who walk not after the flesh, but after the Spirit.***

We are not only free from the *penalty of sin,* we are free from the *power of sin* because of *God sending His own Son in the likeness of the flesh.* What the Law could not do, Jesus did! The Law cannot give us the energy or the power to live the kingdom life, but *the Spirit of life in Christ* Jesus can. Through Jesus being identified with us and taking on the *likeness of sinful flesh (not sinful flesh),* He defeated all of the sins that are against us on the cross. How? God the Eternal Spirit came as God the Son in a body that was *prepared* for Him to fulfill the Law and then die for those who could not keep the Law. Study these verses and let the Spirit that inspired the Holy Bible explain:

> ***Wherefore when he cometh into the world, he saith, Sacrifice and offering thou wouldest not, but a body hast thou prepared me: In burnt offerings and sacrifices for sin thou hast had no pleasure. Then said I, Lo, I come (in the volume of the book it is written of me,) to do thy will, O God. Above when he said, Sacrifice and offering and burnt offerings and offering for sin thou wouldest not, neither hadst pleasure therein; which are offered by the law; Then said he, Lo, I come to do thy will, O God. He taketh away the first, that he may establish the second. By the which will we are sanctified through the offering of the body of Jesus Christ once for all.*** **Hebrews 10:5-10**

> ***Blotting out the handwriting of ordinances that was against us, which was contrary to us, and took it out of the way, nailing it to his cross.*** **Colossians 2:14**

"That the righteousness of the law might be fulfilled in us, who walk not after the flesh, but after the Spirit." - Notice how carefully Paul chooses his words here. He does not say that we fulfill the righteous requirement of the Law, but the *righteous requirement of the Law is fulfilled in us*. It is not *by us,* but *in us*. It is the supernatural work of the Holy Spirit within us! God wants the Holy Spirit to rule in our lives. The course of life and the progress of our life are directed by the Holy Spirit. The Holy Spirit has liberated us from obeying the flesh. Again, this all begins when we are baptized in the Holy Spirit at the born again experience. Just as Paul, each individual must claim his or her own victory.

Conflict of the Spirit and the Flesh

> **Romans 8:5-8 - *For they that are after the flesh do mind the things of the flesh; but they that are after the Spirit the things of the Spirit. For to be carnally minded is death; but to be spiritually minded is life and peace. Because the carnal mind is enmity against God: for it is not subject to the law of God, neither indeed can be. So then they that are in the flesh cannot please God.***

The key word in this passage is the *mind*, or the Greek *phroneo.* What is the intent of our *minds*? What do we keep our *minds* on most of the time? A carnal mind leads to *death*, and a spiritual mind leads to *life and peace.* Even if our *minds* are set with good intentions, we can still be *carnally minded.* The *carnally-minded* person may try to live right and do good to others, while at the same time think that * God is in debt to him.

★ *(One older gentleman said that he had lived a good life, raised a big family, and worked hard all of his life. He did not believe that God would let him go to hell. This is an example of a carnally-minded person.)*

"So then they that are in the flesh cannot please God." - The word *please* here is *aresko* and it means *"being willing to serve."* This carries with it the idea that the *flesh cannot please God,* but that *walking in the Spirit can please God.* It would be glorious if we all had a testimony where we tried to *please God*!

> ***By faith Enoch was translated that he should not see death; and was not found, because God had translated him: for before his translation he had this testimony,*** *that he pleased God*. **Hebrews 11:5**

Empowered the Holy Spirit

> **Romans 8:9-11** - ***But ye are not in the flesh, but in the Spirit, if so be that the Spirit of God dwell in you. Now if any man have not the Spirit of Christ, he is none of his. And if Christ be in you, the body is dead because of sin; but the Spirit is life because of righteousness. But if the Spirit of him that raised up Jesus from the dead dwell in you, he that raised up Christ from the dead shall also quicken your mortal bodies by his Spirit that dwelleth in you.***

Here Paul lets the believers in Rome know that the very same Spirit that raised Yeshua/Jesus *from the dead* is the

Spirit that gives them power over the flesh. This is the Spirit that lives within the hearts of believers. If anyone does not have the Spirit within him that *raised up Jesus from the dead, then he has never been truly born again. He that raised up Christ from the dead shall also quicken your mortal bodies by his Spirit that dwelleth in you.* Our bodies become the Temple of God. Let us take a moment to see how this connects the locations of the *Spirit of God* in the Old and New Testaments:

> ***Then a cloud covered the tent of the congregation, and the glory of the Lord filled the tabernacle. And Moses was not able to enter into the tent of the congregation, because the cloud abode thereon, and the glory of the Lord filled the tabernacle.*** **Exodus 40:34-35** *(Tabernacle)*
>
> ***And it came to pass, when the priests were come out of the holy place, that the cloud filled the house of the Lord, So that the priests could not stand to minister because of the cloud: for the glory of the Lord had filled the house of the Lord.*** **I Kings 8:10-11** *(Solomon's Temple)*
>
> ***For in him dwelleth all the fulness of the Godhead bodily.*** **Colossians 2:9** *(Body of Jesus)*
>
> ***Know ye not that ye are the temple of God, and that the Spirit of God dwelleth in you?*** **I Corinthians 3:16** *(Body of a Christian)*

The Spirit that moved over the face of the waters in **Genesis 1:2** is the same Spirit that brings about a new creation when we place our sincere faith in the Risen Christ! Wow! This is how we live a *life of righteousness* and overcome the flesh!

★ ***Did the Holy Spirit draw you to Jesus?***

★ ***Did the Holy Spirit give you the desire to live for Jesus?***

★ ***Did the Holy Spirit give you the desire to study His Word?***

★ ***Did the Holy Spirit give you the desire to be like Jesus?***

★ ***Are you being filled with the Spirit daily?*** **(Ephesians 5:18)**

★ *(Some ministers of the gospel have done a great injustice by telling people to make a decision for Christ when it was just an emotional experience, or telling them that if they get water baptized and join the church that is enough. This has given countless people the false security that they are Christians, and then they find out later in life that they were never truly born again. Our job is to be faithful to preach God's Word in context and trust the Holy Spirit to touch the people. Without the Holy Spirit, there are no real conversions, and there is no way to live the Christian life.)*

> **Romans 8:12-13 -** ***Therefore, brethren, we are debtors, not to the flesh, to live after the flesh. For if ye live after the flesh, ye shall die: but if ye through the Spirit do mortify the deeds of the body, ye shall live.***

The flesh gives us nothing good and stands in rebellion against God even after we are saved. We have no obligation to pamper the flesh. There are many Christians, like the Galatians, who start out following Christ and then they get entangled again with the Law and fall back into living their lives in the flesh. Or they may become carnal Christians like the believers were in **I Corinthians 3:1-3,** who were babes in Christ and focused on certain apostles, preachers, and gifts and could not be taught the deeper things of Christ.

But we *can live* and enjoy the eternal life we have in Christ through allowing the *Holy Spirit to mortify the deeds of the body.* We do not owe the flesh anything, but *we are in* ★ *debt to the Holy Spirit.*

★ *("Holy Spirit breathe on me, until my heart is clean, let sunshine fill its inmost part without a cloud between. Breathe on me, breathe on me, Holy Spirit breathe on me, take my heart, cleanse every part, Holy Spirit breathe on me" - B. B. McKinney 1937)*

A Believer in Christ is a Child of God

> **Romans 8:14-15 -** ***For as many as are led by the Spirit of God, they are the sons of God. For ye have not received the spirit of bondage again to fear; but ye have received the Spirit of adoption, whereby we cry, Abba, Father.***

Walking in the Spirit here is described as being *led by the Spirit of God.* Being *led by the Spirit of God* is not a pre-condition to being a *son of God.* We become *sons of God* first, and then *the Spirit of God leads us.* Paul's words did not say if we read our Bible, attend Bible study, attend church services, or take communion that we automatically become the *sons of God.*

How does the Spirit of God lead us?

* ***By showing us His will as we study His Word***
* ***The Spirit of God guides us with His wisdom and understanding***
* ***The Spirit of God draws us to a closer walk with Christ***
* ***The Spirit of God reveals Christ to us in a deeper way* - (John 15:26)**
* ***The Spirit of God gives us the power to lead others***
* ***The Spirit of God convicts us and leads us to repentance***
* ***The Spirit of God leads us to think less of ourselves***
* ***The Spirit of God leads us into all truth***
* ***The Spirit of Gods leads us into a life of peace, joy, and love***
* ***The Spirit of God leads us into a life of holiness***
* ***The Spirit of God leads us to find our purpose in God's service***

Notice the Spirit of God leads us, He does not drive us. When Jesus cast the demons out of the maniac of Gadara, the demons entered into the swine and violently drove them into the sea. **(Mark 5:13)** Whenever a person is a fanatic or a radical about religion, *the Spirit of Christ* is not leading that individual.

***"For ye have not received the spirit of bondage again to fear; but ye have received the Spirit of adoption, whereby we cry, Abba, Father."* -** The children of Israel were called both "sons" and "servants." **(Deut. 14:1, Lev. 25:55)** The status of a son was considered to be higher than a servant. Notice Paul uses the words *spirit of bondage again to fear.* The new life in Christ is not a reiteration of the life under the Law. The Holy Spirit did not place the believer in Christ under the Law *again*!

The Law would say *"I must do this,"* while being led by the Spirit of God says, *"I want to do this."* A child of God does not live in the *bondage of fear:*

> ***For God hath not given us the spirit of fear; but of power, and of love, and of a sound mind.*** **2 Timothy 1:7**

The Greek word for *adoption* is *huiothesias*, and it means *"a son into a divine family."* The status of a son of God means that we can ***"cry out, Abba Father."*** It is interesting here that while Paul was writing in Greek, he used the Aramaic/ Hebrew word *"Abba"* probably because of the seriousness of us being able to call ⋆ God our Father! The words *"Abba, Father"* is used two other times in the New Testament, including once by Jesus Himself:

> ***And he said, Abba, Father, all things are possible unto thee; take away this cup from me: nevertheless not what I will, but what thou wilt.*** **Mark 14:36**
>
> ***And because ye are sons, God hath sent forth the Spirit of his Son into your hearts, crying, Abba, Father.*** **Galatians 4:6**

⋆ *(On the Mt. of Beatitudes in Galilee there was a carved stone found on the lower slope with a face of Jesus, and the Hebrew letters above that reads, "Our Father in heaven." Because of Jesus coming into the world, we can have a personal relationship with God as our Father. "After this manner therefore pray ye: Our Father which art in heaven."* **Matthew 6:9)**

Romans 8:16 - ***The Spirit itself beareth witness with our spirit, that we are the children of God:***

Because we have been born again by the Holy Spirit, *He bears witness with our spirit that we are a child of God!* When we read the Sacred Scriptures that were inspired by the Holy Spirit, He gives us the peace and assurance that we belong to God. We do not have to live in doubt and confusion if we are saved. God's children know who they are because He knows us:

> ***The Lord is my shepherd; I shall not want.*** **Psalm 23:1**
>
> ***My sheep hear my voice, and I know them, and they follow me:*** **John 10:27**

Under Jewish law there had to be the mouth of two or three witnesses. **(Deut. 17:6)** God the Father knows us, Jesus the Son of God knows us, the Holy Spirit knows us, and THEY witness to our spirit.

> ***Jesus answered and said unto him, If a man love me, he will keep my words: and my Father will love him, and we will come unto him, and make our abode with him.*** **John 14:23**

Benefits and Responsibilities

Romans 8:17 - ***And if children, then heirs; heirs of God, and joint-heirs with Christ; if so be that we suffer with him, that we may be also glorified together.***

Because we are *in Christ,* we have the benefit of relating to the Father as Jesus does. Therefore, we are *heirs of God and joint heirs with Christ.* What a statement! Being an *heir of God* is not based upon our performance, but based upon our faith in Jesus Christ and His finished work. Notice the progression that Paul has given us from **Romans 4:**

* ***Child of Abraham***
* ***Sons of God***
* ***Heirs of God***
* ***Joint heirs with Christ***

"if so be that we suffer with him, that we may be also glorified together" - As Jesus suffered on the cross, we too have a cross to carry. **(Matthew 16:24)** Because we have been spiritually baptized into His death, burial, and resurrection, we must realize that the world hated Him, and the world will hate us as well. Being a child of God does not mean that we are immune from trials and *suffering.* Jesus gave the *Parable of the Mysteries of the Kingdom* in **Matthew 13** and within the *Parable of the Sower* **(Matthew 13:5, 13:20-21)** some of the seed fell on *stony places* which meant that when persecution and *suffering* arose, they dropped out.

One of the things that causes a stumbling block in many Christian's lives is the curse of this fallen world. In a fallen world that is unfair, sometimes the wicked prosper and the righteous suffer. **(Psalm 73)** We have to remember that there is a payday coming. If we *suffer* because we are following Jesus and people ridicule us and persecute us, *one day we will be glorified with Christ.* We cannot have the *glory* without the *suffering.* One day we will be with Christ and be free from sin, suffering, corruption, and death. There is ⋆ *suffering* in this world and *glory* in the world to come!

⋆ (And God shall wipe away all tears from their eyes; and there shall be no more death, neither sorrow, nor crying, neither shall there be any more pain: for the former things are passed away. **Revelation 21:4)**

> **Romans 8:18 - *For I reckon that the sufferings of this present time are not worthy to be compared with the glory which shall be revealed in us.***

Although the *sufferings of this present time* often seem dreadful and nearly unbearable, they are dwarfed when *compared* to the greatness of the glory to which they will lead. Paul wrote these words to the believers in Corinth:

> ***For our light affliction, which is but for a moment, worketh for us a far more exceeding and eternal weight of glory.* 2 Corinthians 4:17**

As we will see, Paul is not only thinking of the individual person, but rather of our participation in the glorious transformation of the entire creation. We have the glory within us now, but it will be *revealed* one day. This truth really echoes what was written in the *Psalms* in the words of Jesus:

> ***But the meek shall inherit the earth; and shall delight themselves in the abundance of peace.* Psalm 37:11**
>
> ***Blessed are the poor in spirit: for theirs is the kingdom of heaven. Blessed are they that mourn: for they shall***

be comforted. Blessed are the meek: for they shall inherit the earth. **Matthew 5:3-5**

Creation is Awaiting the Coming Glory

Romans 8:19-22 - ***For the earnest expectation of the creature waiteth for the manifestation of the sons of God. For the creature was made subject to vanity, not willingly, but by reason of him who hath subjected the same in hope, Because the creature itself also shall be delivered from the bondage of corruption into the glorious liberty of the children of God. For we know that the whole creation groaneth and travaileth in pain together until now.***

The Greek word for *"earnest expectation"* is one word, *apokaradokia,* and it means *"not only looking for but intensely yearning."* This wording correlates with the Hebrew wording in this verse in *Psalms:*

As the hart panteth after the water brooks, so panteth (ta arog) my soul after thee, O God. Psalm 42:1

The writer of the book of *Hebrews* describes this glorious day by saying it belongs to the ones who are *looking for* Christ to appear.

So Christ was once offered to bear the sins of many; and unto them that look for him shall he appear the second time without sin unto salvation. **Hebrews 9:28**

Creation was *subject to vanity not willingly* as a result of man's sin. Creation cannot enjoy its redemption until the glory of *the sons of God is manifested.* When God's children are released from the bondage of corruption, then all of nature will be released. We as followers of Christ are to live in this fallen world grounded in *the hope* that God has promised.

Well over a thousand verses in the Sacred Scriptures directly refer to the coming kingdom when Jesus will be King over all the earth in the Davidic Kingdom. It is so sad that we hear very few sermons about the Kingdom Age that is to come because of anti-Semitism and certain denominational doctrines that over-spiritualize those scriptures and refuse to accept the fact that Jesus will return *to Jerusalem* and set up the 1,000-year reign. **(Zechariah 14, Matthew 19:28, Revelation 20:6)** If we can see such beauty in God's creation now, *how much more* will it be when the day of redemption comes? Again, we would be better served to allow the scriptures to explain themselves.

> ***And unto Adam he said, Because thou hast hearkened unto the voice of thy wife, and hast eaten of the tree, of which I commanded thee, saying, Thou shalt not eat of it: cursed is the ground for thy sake; in sorrow shalt thou eat of it all the days of thy life; Thorns also and thistles shall it bring forth to thee; and thou shalt eat the herb of the field; In the sweat of thy face shalt thou eat bread, till thou return unto the ground; for out of it wast thou taken: for dust thou art, and unto dust shalt thou return.*** **Genesis 3:17-19**
>
> ***The wolf also shall dwell with the lamb, and the leopard shall lie down with the kid; and the calf and the young lion and the fatling together; and a little***

> ***child shall lead them. And the cow and the bear shall feed; their young ones shall lie down together: and the lion shall eat straw like the ox. And the sucking child shall play on the hole of the asp, and the weaned child shall put his hand on the cockatrice' den. They shall not hurt nor destroy in all my holy mountain: for the earth shall be full of the knowledge of the Lord, as the waters cover the sea.*** **Isaiah 11:6-9**

What we are seeing today that is happening in a world filled with earthquakes, hurricanes, tornadoes, famine, pestilence, and change in weather patterns are birth pangs of the messianic age to come. All of *creation is groaning* for its redemption.

> **Romans 8:23-25 -** ***And not only they, but ourselves also, which have the firstfruits of the Spirit, even we ourselves groan within ourselves, waiting for the adoption, to wit, the redemption of our body. For we are saved by hope: but hope that is seen is not hope: for what a man seeth, why doth he yet hope for? But if we hope for that we see not, then do we with patience wait for it.***

This is an interesting passage where the Hebrew thought of *"firstfruits"* is used as a metaphor for man's present redemption and future resurrection. The *firstfruits*, or the Hebrew *bikkurim*, are the first of the produce that is offered at the Feast of Pentecost. **(Exo.23:16, Numbers 28:26)** Since God's gift of the Holy Spirit cleanses man from the sins of the flesh and gives him the inheritance of eternal life, "we" become *spiritual offerings* one might say. When we are walking in the Spirit, we even manifest the *fruits of the Spirit.* **(Galatians 5:22)** What the Holy Spirit has done in the life of the believer in Christ is the *firstfruits* of what will follow in the glorification and resurrection. They represent the guarantee of eternal life! What we are experiencing now is just a taste of what is to come!

Although we have already been adopted into God's family, we are waiting for the consummation of our *adoption, which will happen at the redemption of the body.*

> ***For this corruptible must put on incorruption, and this mortal must put on immortality.*** **I Corinthians 15:53**

"For we are saved by hope: but hope that is seen is not hope: for what a man seeth, why doth he yet hope for? But if we hope for that we see not, then do we with patience wait for it." - Notice how many times the word *hope* is used here. The Greek word for *hope* is *elpis* and it means *"anticipate."* The English word for *hope* means *"desiring for a certain thing to happen."* Neither the Greek nor the English carry the strength and power of the Hebrew thought. The Hebrew word for *hope* is *tiqvah*, and it means *"the binding of a cord or rope."* No doubt the Jewish Apostle Paul had the Hebrew thought in mind. *Hope* in Hebrew is not just wishful thinking, or hoping that something will happen one day. We are *bound together* with God by our faith in Christ, and our eternal life is a sure thing even though we cannot *see* the future. Notice this idea in the *Psalms:*

> ***My soul*** *(nephesh)*, ***wait thou only upon God*** *(Elohim)*; ***for my expectation*** *(tiqvah)* ***is from him.*** **Psalm 62:5**

The Holy Spirit Helps Us to Pray

> **Romans 8:26-27 - *Likewise the Spirit also helpeth our infirmities: for we know not what we should pray for as we ought: but the Spirit itself maketh intercession for us with groanings which cannot be uttered. And he that searcheth the hearts knoweth what is the mind of the Spirit, because he maketh intercession for the saints according to the will of God.***

Paul uses the plural form of *"groaneth," sustenazo,* in verse 22, when all of creation is *groaning* for its redemption. Here he uses the singular form *stenagnos*, which can mean a *groan or a sigh.* Because we live in a fallen world that is yearning for the Second Coming of Christ to lift the curse, we face disappointments and trials and sorrows that come sometimes. When we pray, we do not always have the words to express what we want to say. We just *groan and sigh,* and no one seems to understand, but the Holy Spirit knows our hearts. Even David, centuries ago, felt this deep *groaning* when he prayed:

> ***Lord, all my desire is before thee; and my groaning*** *(Hebrew anachah, for sighing or groaning)* ***is not hid from thee.* Psalm 38:9**

Even our Lord Jesus *sighed* on several occasions, and once when He prayed just before touching a man who was deaf and had an impediment in his speech:

And looking up to heaven, he sighed, and saith unto him, Ephphatha, that is, Be opened. **Mark 7:34**

Since all of creation is *groaning* with us, it has been proven that sometimes animals and flowers know when we are sad. The ★ silent scream that we feel from time to time is when we need the Holy Spirit to intercede for us. The *courts of heaven* are listening, and they bring us comfort in those most difficult times. The Holy Spirit not only *leads* along this spiritual journey, but He helps us to *pray*; being the Third Person of the Triune Godhead, He knows the will of God.

★ *(God understands our language when we do not have the words to pray. This can include the nights we cannot sleep and just need to talk to God; the times we look up into the stars and just need a touch from heaven; when reading the Holy Bible and we are filled with a holy hush, and just praise the Lord from our innermost being. Jesus the Son of God walked this earth and finished His mission and is now seated at the right hand of God in heaven. The Holy Spirit is at work <u>now</u> in the world helping and aiding the believer in Jesus.* **John 16:7-11)**

The idea that the Lord shines His light into our lives and searches our innermost parts is found in many places in the Bible:

The spirit of man is the candle of the Lord, searching all the inward parts of the belly. **Proverbs 20:27**

(Yea, a sword shall pierce through thy own soul also,) that the thoughts of many hearts may be revealed. **Luke 2:35**

God is Working Through All Things

> **Romans 8:28-30** - ***And we know that all things work together for good to them that love God, to them who are the called according to his purpose. For whom he did foreknow, he also did predestinate to be conformed to the image of his Son, that he might be the firstborn among many brethren. Moreover whom he did predestinate, them he also called: and whom he called, them he also justified: and whom he justified, them he also glorified.***

Another basis for our ability to endure suffering is found in the *purpose of God.* In this fallen world, God is at work even when we do not realize it. This passage has been misunderstood and used as *just* an individual's positive interpretation that *"everything is going to be alright."* It needs to be interpreted that *"all things,"* or the Greek *pas,* meaning *every kind of, the whole of creation combined* with our own experiences are working toward a splendid goal, the age to come! *All of creation is working together for good with them who love God.* When we suffer, we are participating in God's larger goal in preparing for the glorious day to come. Christian suffering is a part of the cosmic drama that is unfolding at the present time that will ultimately lead to glorification.

This passage is *not* talking about the suffering that we bring upon ourselves through the bad choices that we make. It is referring to the sufferings of those *who love God and who are led by the Spirit.* As we serve Christ, we will suffer persecution and disappointments, but God is working through everything to bring us to a closer relationship with Him and one day make us in *the image of His Son.* Jesus Christ is the center of God's purpose and plan. God's creation and those *who love the Lord* have a glorious freedom in the future from bondage and corruption.

"For whom he did foreknow, *(Greek proginosko, to know beforehand)* **he also did predestinate** *(Greek proorizo, foreordain)* ***to be conformed to the image of his Son, that he might be the firstborn among many brethren. Moreover whom he did predestinate, them he also called:*** *(Greek kaleo, "I call, invite, summons)* ***and whom he called, them he also justified:*** *(Greek dikaioo, to show to be righteous)* ***and whom he justified, them he also glorified,*** *(Greek doxazo, to render glorious)*" – This *eternal chain* of a plethora of verbs have caused serious divisions in the body of Christ regarding different theologies of the Christian churches. We will try to put it into words for better understanding. The Almighty God, who is the Supreme, Sovereign Ruler of His Creation, set a plan in motion long before time began. A *general invitation* or *call* would be given to the *whole world* to accept His plan of salvation through His Son Jesus. Jesus was even *foreordained* to be crucified before the world began. (I Peter 1:20) Just because the Eternal God is *omniscient (all-knowing)* and knew beforehand who would accept His invitation does not mean that He *arbitrarily* picked who would be saved and who would not. ⋆ Everyone who would *freely* accept the Lord Jesus Christ would be filled with His Holy Spirit. The Eternal God *foreordained* they would one day be *justified*, and one day be glorified, and be made like His Son Jesus.

⋆ *(The idea that God chose some to go to heaven and desired others to go to hell (or double predestination) goes against countless verses in the Holy Bible. We will look further into this thought when we get to the word "election" in* **Romans 9-11.** *While there certainly are mysteries in the Divine Counsels of God that we finite humans cannot understand, we need to compare scriptures and allow God's Word to give us the true interpretations. If our interpretation of a passage of scripture is contradicted in some other place in the Bible, then we can know that our interpretation is wrong. The scriptures teach man's free will and responsibility to receive Christ while also teaching that God foreknew the ones who would be saved. There is no contradiction! God desired for all to be saved! Worship is not worship if it is dictated or forced upon anyone. Here are a few verses to carefully study:)*

> ***Say unto them, As I live, saith the Lord God, I have no pleasure in the death of the wicked; but that the wicked turn from his way and live: turn ye, turn ye from your evil ways; for why will ye die, O house of Israel?*** **Ezekiel 33:11**
>
> ***That was the true Light, which lighteth every man that cometh into the world.*** **John 1:9**
>
> ***For God so loved the world, that he gave his only begotten Son, that whosoever believeth in him should not perish, but have everlasting life. For God sent not his Son into the world to condemn the world; but that the world through him might be saved.*** **John 3:16-17**
>
> ***He that believeth on the Son hath everlasting life: and he that believeth not the Son shall not see life; but the wrath of God abideth on him.*** **John 3:36**

> *And ye will not come to me, that ye might have life.* **John 5:40**
>
> *And he said unto them, Go ye into all the world, and preach the gospel to every creature.* **Mark 16:15**
>
> *Who will have all men to be saved, and to come unto the knowledge of the truth.* **I Timothy 2:4**
>
> *The Lord is not slack concerning his promise, as some men count slackness; but is longsuffering to us-ward, not willing that any should perish, but that all should come to repentance.* **2 Peter 3:9**
>
> *And he is the propitiation for our sins: and not for ours only, but also for the sins of the whole world.* **I John 2:2**
>
> *And the Spirit and the bride say, Come. And let him that heareth say, Come. And let him that is athirst come. And whosoever will, let him take the water of life freely.* **Revelation 22:17**

"that he might be the firstborn among many brethren." **-** Jesus Christ is not only the center of the *purpose of God,* He is also the *Preeminent Heir* with *many brethren* who are also *heirs.* God has *predetermined* for us that one day we will share in the likeness of the *Firstborn Heir.* This actually confirms our eternal security, because our eternal salvation is all based on the finished work of Christ and the Father answering His Son's prayer in **John 17,** that accomplished the Divine Plan that was set in motion *before the foundation of the world.* God predetermined that all who accepted His Son Jesus would one day be made like Him!

> ***Father, I will that they also, whom thou hast given me, be with me where I am; that they may behold my glory, which thou hast given me: for thou lovedst me before the foundation of the world.*** **John 17:24**

This idea of Jesus being *the firstborn among many brethren* goes back to **Romans 8:17,** where *if we co-suffer with Him we shall also be co-glorified with Him.*

> ***Beloved, now are we the sons of God, and it doth not yet appear what we shall be: but we know that, when he shall appear, we shall be like him; for we shall see him as he is.*** **I John 3:2**

GREAT ENCOURAGEMENT

> **Romans 8:31 -** ***What shall we then say to these things? If God be for us, who can be against us?***

Since the Almighty God of the Universe has *foreordained* that all who believe in Jesus will be *called, justified, and one day glorified,* and all that Jesus went through to save us, who can doubt that *God is for us*? We can take enormous comfort in the reality that our relationship to God stretches from eternity past to eternity future. *God is only on the side of the Jews or Gentiles* who have been reconciled to Him through faith in Christ. We can endure suffering when we know that *God is for us.* There are cultists and terrorists that claim that God is with them, but God is only for those who are *in Christ.* Who can fight against The Lord God Almighty and win?

Romans 8:32 - ***He that spared not his own Son, but delivered him up for us all, how shall he not with him also freely give us all things?***

The ultimate proof of God's unconditional love for Israel and for the Church is the gift of *Yeshua/Jesus,* His only begotten Son. If God would *deliver,* or the Greek *paredoken,* ⋆ *turn over* Jesus, to suffer the eternal consequences of *our* sins, will He not graciously give *us* freely a share in all of the glory that His Son will have in the messianic kingdom and in heaven? All believers in Christ will be given a share in the ⋆⋆ *glorious creation* that will be renewed, plus the very eternal life of Jesus Christ. If God would give us the *ultimate Gift,* how much more will He give us the *smaller gifts?*

⋆ ***For to do whatsoever thy hand and thy counsel determined before to be done.*** **Acts 4:28**

⋆⋆ ***Nevertheless we, according to his promise, look for new heavens and a new earth, wherein dwelleth righteousness.*** **2 Peter 3:13**

Security of the Believer in God's Love

Romans 8:33-39 - ***Who shall lay any thing to the charge of God's elect? It is God that justifieth. Who is he that condemneth? It is Christ that died, yea rather, that is risen again, who is even at the right hand of God, who also maketh intercession for us. Who shall separate us from the love of Christ? shall tribulation, or distress, or persecution, or famine,***

> ***or nakedness, or peril, or sword? As it is written, For thy sake we are killed all the day long; we are accounted as sheep for the slaughter. Nay, in all these things we are more than conquerors through him that loved us. For I am persuaded, that neither death, nor life, nor angels, nor principalities, nor powers, nor things present, nor things to come, Nor height, nor depth, nor any other creature, shall be able to separate us from the love of God, which is in Christ Jesus our Lord.***

If we have been *elected (because we accepted Christ)* and *justified* by the highest Judge in the Universe, who is now our *Abba Father,* how can anyone bring any additional charges against us? If we have been declared righteous through the blood of God's only Son, how can anyone else *condemn* us? *It is Christ who died and rose again* and is in heaven at this present hour making *intercession* for His people. *(This is the only time in Paul's writings where he refers to the intercessory work of Christ on our behalf in the presence of God.)* In the court of heaven, no accuser has any standing because Christ died and rose again. The resurrection of Christ brought *life* to us, not *rejection.* Notice these very familiar verses again that were spoken by our Lord Jesus:

> ***For God so loved the world, that he gave his only begotten Son, that whosoever believeth in him should not perish, but have everlasting life. For God sent not his Son into the world to condemn the world; but that the world through him might be saved. He that believeth on him is not condemned:***

> ***but he that believeth not is condemned already, because he hath not believed in the name of the only begotten Son of God.*** **John 3:16-18**

Satan will do everything he can to make us feel guilty, and even our own conscience sometimes tries to *condemn* us.

> ***For if our heart condemn us, God is greater than our heart, and knoweth all things.*** **I John 3:20**

"Who shall separate us from the love of Christ? shall tribulation, or distress, or persecution, or famine, or nakedness, or peril, or sword? As it is written, For thy sake we are killed all the day long; we are accounted as sheep for the slaughter. Nay, in all these things we are more than conquerors through him that loved us." **-** Notice that Paul explicitly refers for the first time in Romans to *the love of Christ,* which is the same thing as *the love of God.* Since Christ is the One who died and rose again, it is appropriate to refer to His personal love *for us.* Jesus is not just a disinterested defense attorney - His death on the tree was motivated by *His love for us*! Paul uses a choice of words here that suggests a wide range of experiences that also have their own particular emphasis:

* ***Tribulation-distress (general words)***
* ***Persecution- famine- nakedness- peril (Various forms of tribulation)***

"As it is written" refers to **Psalm 44** where even in Israel's defeat and disgrace, God would search this out:

> ***If we have forgotten the name of our God, or stretched out our hands to a strange god; Shall not God search***

this out? for he knoweth the secrets of the heart. ***Yea, for thy sake are we killed all the day long; we are counted as sheep for the slaughter.*** **Psalm 44:20-22**

Sometimes our suffering as believers in Christ is a result of our own choices, sometimes the results of carrying the cross for Jesus, and sometimes the suffering is unexplainable in a fallen world. *We are more than conquerors through him that loved us! Hallelujah!* Through the victory we have in Christ, we have a greater power, a greater motive, and a greater love that our enemies cannot understand and do not have.

"For I am persuaded, that neither death, nor life, nor angels, nor principalities, nor powers, nor things present, nor things to come, Nor height, nor depth, nor any other creature, shall be able to separate us from the love of God, which is in Christ Jesus our Lord." - Paul is firmly and completely *persuaded* that nothing can separate him from the Divine love of Christ.

- ***Death nor life*** - (Not anything in our experience of living or when this life ends)
- ***Principalities nor powers*** - (No evil supernatural being whatever its position)
- ***Things present or things to come*** - (Not anything today or in the future)
- ***Height, nor depth*** - (Not anything at the highest or lowest level of existence)
- ***Any other creature*** - (Created beings in hell or wherever they may be, **Ephesians 1:19-23, Philippians 2:9-11**)

The reason why nothing can *separate us from the love of God, which is in Christ Jesus our Lord,* is because He is in heaven as the Risen, Glorified Christ, and has absolute power over every experience in our lives. Would Christ have died that horrible death on the tree and have gone down into the lower parts of the earth on our behalf and then separate Himself from us? We may drift away from Christ, even fall into sin *(not habitual sin),* and may lose our rewards **(I Cor. 3:12-15),** but our eternal security is not performance based. It is based on the love of Christ!

CHAPTER NINE

Has God Rejected Israel?

In these next three chapters we find a shift in focus to the book of Romans. These three chapters hold verses that many within Christendom today still either reject or refuse to accept, or take them out of context for their own interpretation. We would be wise to approach these three chapters with caution and ask the Holy Spirit to give us discernment. We have been convinced through the first eight chapters about man's needs and God's glorious provision in Jesus Christ and how to live the Christian life through the Holy Spirit. We must remind ourselves that the believers in Rome were a mixed group of Jews and Gentiles, and now Paul deals with the problem associated with the ⋆ unbelieving Jews or Israel. What does it mean that Israel as a nation has missed its Messiah? Because most of Israel is in unbelief, can the Jewish believers in Christ be secure in their salvation? What about all the promises that God made to Israel in the Old Testament? What about some of the words that even the Lord Jesus gave?

And Jesus said unto them, Verily I say unto you, That ye which have followed me, in the regeneration when the Son of man shall sit in the throne of his glory, ye also shall sit upon twelve thrones, judging the twelve tribes of Israel. **Matthew 19:28**

When they therefore were come together, they asked of him, saying, Lord, wilt thou at this time restore again the kingdom to Israel? And he said unto them, It is not for you to know the times or the seasons, which the Father hath put in his own power. Acts 1:6-7

★ *(When the Roman Emperor Constantine legalized the practice of Christianity in 313AD, the Jews had been expelled from the Land of Israel, and most of them were still unbelievers. Constantine failed to recognize, or did not want to recognize, that Jesus was a Jew* **(Matthew 1:1, John 4:9)** *and the first followers of Jesus Christ were Jews.* **(Acts 2:5, Romans 1:16)** *Constantine also failed to see that salvation came to the world through the Jews.* **(John 4:22)** *Therefore, the Catholic Church began a Gentile form of Christianity and taught that God was finished with the Jews. The scriptures referring to God's promises to Israel were over-spiritualized and given to the Church, or Gentile Christians. This anti-Semitism was carried over to the Reformation leaders like Martin Luther, who wrote such hateful words about the Jews that are too horrible to even mention. The devil used this misplacement-of-scripture doctrine to play a big, "religious" part in the Holocaust and the killing of over 6 million Jews between 1933-1945.)*

Romans 9:1-3 - ***I say the truth in Christ, I lie not, my conscience also bearing me witness in the Holy***

Ghost, That I have great heaviness and continual sorrow in my heart. For I could wish that myself were accursed from Christ for my brethren, my kinsmen according to the flesh:

The Jewish Paul gave us such a glorious thought in **Romans 8,** that nothing shall separate us from the love of God. Then Paul acquires a very somber tone when talking about his great sorrow over unbelieving Israel. Paul wants the believers in Rome to make no mistake about how serious he feels about the unbelieving Jews. We should note the ⋆ double affirmations here:

⋆ ***I say the truth in Christ - I lie not***

⋆ ***My conscience – the Holy Ghost***

As we will see, chapters 9-11 confirm that Paul's attitude toward Israel is predicated on what the Sacred Scriptures reveal about Israel's relationship to God. Paul's feelings are not just some emotional attachment, but are a result of the Holy Spirit working within him about his own *kinsmen according to the flesh.*

Paul uses the Greek word *odune* for *sorrow* here. It actually appears in the sense of *pain* in Greek medical literature. Try to imagine Paul being a Jew himself who had been called by the Lord Jesus Christ to take the message to the Gentiles, and along the way some of his brethren would receive Christ, but the majority of the Jews would not. His compassion to see the Jews saved is even deepened because of their hostility toward the gospel. Paul's heart does not turn bitter or is filled with hate, but rather he has a broken heart for his own people.

"For I could wish that myself were accursed** (Greek anathema) **from Christ for my brethren, my kinsmen according to the flesh" **-** This verse has been taught that Paul was willing to go to hell for Israel. The word *anathema* is not specific here and can be realized in many different ways. To better understand Paul's words would be *"I could almost wish that I could be cut off from Christ if it would bring salvation to my brethren."* Why? Because Paul knows that the unbelieving Jews are risking being cut off from Christ in eternity and will die in their sins. **(John 8:21-24)** Again, we need to let the scriptures explain themselves. There are times to take the verses literally, and there are other times to read them through the very deep emotions of the person writing. Paul is showing the heart of Jesus for his own *brethren according to the flesh.* Note Paul's heartfelt anguish in later writings and compare it to David's lament and the heart of Moses in the Old Testament:

> ***Therefore I endure all things for the elect's sakes, that they may also obtain the salvation which is in Christ Jesus with eternal glory.*** **2 Timothy 2:10**
>
> ***And the king was much moved, and went up to the chamber over the gate, and wept: and as he went, thus he said, O my son Absalom, my son, my son Absalom! would God I had died for thee, O Absalom, my son, my son!*** **2 Samuel 18:33**
>
> ***And Moses returned unto the Lord, and said, Oh, this people have sinned a great sin, and have made them gods of gold. Yet now, if thou wilt forgive their***

> ***sin--; and if not, blot me, I pray thee, out of thy book which thou hast written.*** **Exodus 32:31-32**

The Privileges of Israel

> **Romans 9:4-5 -** ***Who are Israelites; to whom pertaineth the adoption, and the glory, and the covenants, and the giving of the law, and the service of God, and the promises; Whose are the fathers, and of whom as concerning the flesh Christ came, who is over all, God blessed for ever. Amen.***

Paul's grief for Israel is much more than his being a Jew, but is chiefly founded upon the nation's relationship to God through its Messiah Jesus Christ. Paul wants the Jewish believers in Rome to know how highly favored the nation of Israel is in its people being called *"Israelites."* When God renamed Jacob *"Israel"* in **Genesis 32:28,** that implied the national blessing of Divine favor. Paul uses the term *"Israel"* no less than 12 times in these three chapters and is always referring to the *"Jews,"* which he clearly states in **Romans 9:24.** Paul's grief is much more severe when he considers the blessings that Israel had received from being God's chosen people. This is such a powerful list of privileges that we need to study each one:

"to whom pertaineth the adoption " **-** The national privilege of the nation of Israel parallels the individual *adoption* of the Jewish and Gentile believers that Paul is writing to. Note what God told Moses:

> ***And thou shalt say unto Pharaoh, Thus saith the Lord, Israel is my son, even my firstborn: And I say unto thee, Let my son go, that he may serve me: and if thou refuse to let him go, behold, I will slay thy son, even thy firstborn.*** **Exodus 4:22-23**

"and the glory" - The *Shekinah* glory was manifested to Israel. The Greek word *doxa* does not carry the weight of the Hebrew thought of *kabod*, which was the word that was used throughout the history of Israel in the Old Testament. The *glory*, or *kabod* of God was manifested on *Mt. Sinai,* **(Exo. 24:16-18)** appeared in the *Tabernacle,* **(Exo. 40:34-35)** and when Solomon built the first *Temple.* **(I Kings 8:10-13)**

"and the covenants" - The Greek word for *"covenants"* is "diatheke" while the Hebrew thought of Paul would have been *"beriyth,"* and means *"a sense of cutting"* with the thought of circumcision or of animal sacrifices. While there are five major covenants in the Old Testament; *Noahic, Abrahamic, Mosaic, Davidic, and New Covenant,* Paul probably has in mind the covenants that God gave to Israel starting with Abraham. The New Covenant, which was brought in by the blood of the Messiah, unbelieving Israel refuses to accept.

"and the giving of the law" - Paul is thinking of the privilege that the nation of Israel had when God gave Moses the *Law.* Not just the *Law* in general as Paul refers to in the earlier chapters of Romans, but to all of the numerous commandments and stipulations that flowed from the *Law.* The Greek word for *"Law,"* is *"nomothesia,"* and it means *"legislation."* The Hebrew word and thought for *"Law,"* is

"Torah," and refers to the first five books of the Old Testament written by Moses. Jesus told the religious leaders of His day that if they had believed in Moses' writings, they would have believed in Him, for Moses wrote about Him. **(John 5:46)**

"and the service of God" **-** Only the nation of Israel had a God-ordained system of worship. The elaborate system in the book of *Leviticus* and later in the *Temple* showed Israel how sinful it was and how holy God was. All of the sacrifices pointed to the Messiah who was to come. If they had known the scriptures better, they would have known that Jesus was their Savior when He came.

"and the promises" **-** The Greek word for *"promises,"* is *"eppagelia,"* which means *"a summons."* The Hebrew thought is *"dabar,"* which means *"a declaration that will come to pass."* Paul not only was referring to the many *promises* given to the nation of Israel in a *general* way such as all of the hundreds of verses pertaining to the *promises* of the Davidic Kingdom in the future, but to the *promises* that God gave to the *prophets* concerning the gospel and the coming of the Messiah:

> ***Paul, a servant of Jesus Christ, called to be an apostle, separated unto the gospel of God, (Which he had promised afore by his prophets in the holy scriptures,)***
> **Romans 1:1-2**

"Whose are the fathers, and of whom as concerning the flesh Christ came, * who is over all, God blessed for ever. Amen." **-** This verse is very problematic to those who try to teach that Jesus was not a Jew, or that God has somehow revoked His promises to Israel. The Jews were blessed to have descended from the Patriarchs; Abraham, Isaac, and Jacob. Above all and climactically it must be said that the nation of Israel is the nation from *whom Christ came into the world according to the flesh.* The Savior of the world is the pinnacle of the privileges of the nation of Israel. It is very clear that the Savior of the Gentiles was an Israelite Himself, and Paul did not want them to forget it. Christ was much more than an Israelite. He was God incarnate. Could there be anything more elevating for the Jewish believers in Rome to be reminded of that the Eternal God who rules over everything in the universe became an Israelite? Thus, Paul closes this section with the doxology, *"God blessed forever. Amen."*

★ *(This is a very clear statement, and should be noted to be of great interest. The Apostle Paul declares the deity of Christ! Paul wants the believers in Rome to know that Jesus of Nazareth was not only an Israelite in the flesh, but that He was the God of the universe who rules over everything.)*

Natural and Spiritual Israelites

> **Romans 9:6-7 - *Not as though the word of God hath taken none effect. For they are not all Israel, which are of Israel: Neither, because they are the seed of Abraham, are they all children: but, In Isaac shall thy seed be called.***

Because the majority of Israel is still in unbelief, is not because of any failure with the Word of God. The Greek word for *"none effect"* is *"ekpipto"* and means *"to fall away, or wither away."* The word is used in **I Peter 1:24** for the flower *falling away.*

There have been and still are those who might say, *"God's Word didn't come through for Israel because they missed their Messiah, now they are a cursed people."* Paul is clearly stating that is not the case! Nothing has happened with the unbelieving Jews that will alter God's promises to the nation. An ethnic connection to national *Israel* is not what constitutes spiritual *Israel.* This idea Paul stated earlier in **Romans 2:28, 29.** It is one thing to be an Israelite in the natural sense, and another thing to be a ★ *spiritual Israelite.*

> ***Jesus saw Nathanael coming to him, and saith of him, Behold an Israelite indeed, in whom is no guile!*** **John 1:47**

★ *(A parallel situation is with the word "Christian." Not everyone who is called a "Christian" is a true follower of Christ.)*

"Neither, because they are the seed of Abraham, are they all children: but, In Isaac shall thy seed be called." **-** Just because there is a physical descent from Abraham does not mean they are true children of Abraham. Paul is quoting directly from the Hebrew text in **Genesis 21:12,** when he writes *In Isaac shall thy seed be called.* It is not that God hated the other descendants of Abraham, but His promise was that Jesus Christ would come through *Isaac,* and everyone who accepted Christ would be a true child of Abraham. This did not exclude anyone for salvation, descendants of *Isaac or Ishmael,* who wanted to believe in Jesus. Paul wrote these words concerning the Abrahamic Covenant to the Gentiles:

> ***That the blessing of Abraham might come on the * Gentiles through Jesus Christ; that we might receive the promise of the Spirit through faith. Brethren, I speak after the manner of men; Though it be but a man's covenant, yet if it be confirmed, no man disannulleth, or addeth thereto. Now to Abraham and his seed were the promises made. He saith not, And to seeds, as of many; but as of one, And to thy seed, which is Christ.*** **Galatians 3:14-16**

* *(It does not mean here that the Gentiles took the place of God's promises to Israel, but that they are included, along with the Jews who believe in Jesus, and become children of Abraham when they believe in Jesus Christ. It is only one Messianic promise to Jews and Gentiles! The Jews who believe in Jesus are referred to as the Israel of God in* **Galatians 6:16***.)*

> **Romans 9:8-9** - ***That is, They which are the children of the flesh, these are not the children of God: but the children of the promise are counted for the seed. For this is the word of promise, At this time will I come, and * Sarah shall have a son.***

To be spiritual *children of Abraham* (plural) are to be truly *children of God* (plural), while *children of the flesh* (plural) are not the *children of God* (plural). *Isaac, the son of promise,* was God's direct gift to Abraham through his miraculous birth, when Abraham was too old to beget seed. Like the prototype *Isaac* stands for *the children of promise, Ishmael* is the prototype for the *children of the flesh* who can only speak of a physical connection with Abraham.

★ *(It is very interesting and important here that Paul quotes from* **Genesis 18:9** *and* **18:14.** *Paul is connecting these two verses in Genesis to show the reader of the certainty of Isaac's birth. The promised child had to be a "son" in order to produce an offspring.)*

> **Romans 9:10-13 -** ***And not only this; but when Rebecca also had conceived by one, even by our father Isaac; (For the children being not yet born, neither having done any good or evil, that the purpose of God according to election might stand, not of works, but of him that calleth;) It was said unto her, The elder shall serve the younger. As it is written, ★ Jacob have I loved, but Esau have I hated.***

Paul knew that the question might arise that Isaac and Ishmael had the same father but different mothers. Paul gives a second illustration about *Esau and Jacob.* They both had the same father and the same mother, *Rebecca*; and were even twins. God chose for the Messianic kingdom to be established through *Jacob*, while both of them were still in the womb of *Rebecca.* Paul is alluding to **Genesis 25:23** and quoting from **Malachi 1:2-3.** The *national election of Israel* was determined even before they were born, and had nothing to do with their behavior. When we study the life of Jacob, it is easy to see that his bad behavior certainly had nothing to do with God's choice. God's secrets belong to Him, and His wisdom is past finding out. **(Deut. 29:29)**

★ *(This phrase is not referring to the eternal destiny of either Jacob or Esau; there is no reason not to believe that both of them will be in God's eternal kingdom. God is choosing the vehicle through which the purpose for Israel will be realized. Physical descent is not the basis for God's choice. Ishmael and Esau were both "seed" of Abraham, but neither was the divinely chosen seed from which the nation of Israel would come forth. God was not hostile toward Esau as a person, nor is it referring to the eternal damnation of Esau. Paul is giving the analogy to prove his point about Israel's present condition. The Jews who accept Christ will be blessed like Isaac and Jacob, and those who reject Christ will be vessels of wrath like Ishmael and Esau.)*

In summary through these two illustrations, Paul makes four points:

- ***God's Word has not failed, although Israel has failed***
- ***God's plan is still on course according to His plan***
- ***Spiritual blessings do not come through physical descent, but through God's divine choice*** *(like choosing Israel to bless the nations)*
- ***God's promises are still going to be given to the remnant of Israel who believe in Christ, and to the believing Gentiles***

Is There Unrighteousness With God?

Romans 9:14-16 - ***What shall we say then? Is there unrighteousness with God? God forbid. For he saith to Moses, I will have mercy on whom I will have mercy, and I will have compassion on whom I will have compassion. So then it is not of him that willeth, nor of him that runneth, but of God that sheweth mercy.***

Paul refutes this question again by using the Hebrew idiom *chalilah*, which means *"far be it,"* or *"God forbid."* Paul quotes from **Exodus 33:19** when writing, *"I will have mercy on whom I will have mercy, and I will have compassion on whom I will have compassion."* In the original Hebrew, the words *"chanan"* and *"racham"* for *"mercy and compassion"* are very similar in thought, and both words essentially mean the same thing.

God's mercy is not given to anyone because he deserves it or because of what someone *wills to do,* but simply out of His desire to show mercy. Moses was the meekest man upon the face of the earth **(Numbers 12:3)**, but his meekness did not merit God's mercy. If God was unjust or unrighteous in His dealings with Israel or with the Gentiles, then Paul would have never said, *"I am not ashamed of the gospel of Christ."* **(Romans 1:16)** Looking at things from our perspective on earth, it may seem sometimes that God is not fair. We must remember that the Eternal God knows the beginning from the end, and His ways are much higher than our ways. **(Isaiah 55:8-9)**

God is not obligated to show mercy to anyone or to any nation, but He chose Israel to be the nation to bless the world, and He chose certain individuals to use in the process. In the present time, God has chosen to show mercy on **all** Jews and Gentiles who embrace His Son Jesus. There is nowhere in the Sacred Scriptures where God prevents anyone from believing in Christ by means of some kind of negative predestination in eternity past. Paul would be saddened today to see how many have twisted his words into such a harsh concept. However, no one can come to Christ without the drawing of the Holy

Spirit. These two thoughts must be kept in harmony as we study Romans and the New Testament.

> ***For God, who commanded the light to shine out of darkness, hath shined in our hearts, to give the light of the knowledge of the glory of God in the face of Jesus Christ.*** **2 Corinthians 4:6**

Example of Pharaoh

> **Romans 9:17-18** - ***For the scripture saith unto Pharaoh, Even for this same purpose have I raised thee up, that I might shew my power in thee, and that my name might be declared throughout all the earth. Therefore hath he mercy on whom he will have mercy, and whom he will he hardeneth.***

Paul is quoting from **Exodus 9:16**, and the word in the original Hebrew for *"thee"* is *"raah,"* which means *"to see or to discern."* When God *saw* and knew that the person *Pharaoh* would not believe in Him, He chose to raise *Pharaoh* up for His divine purpose. By doing so, this provided an immediate purpose and a distant purpose. God would show how all-powerful He was over the gods of Egypt and *Pharaoh* through His miracles and the crossing of the Red Sea. While in the future, God's name would be proclaimed in all the earth, and so it has been. Forty years later when Joshua entered into the Promised Land, The Canaanites were still shaking because they had heard of what God had done to Egypt and to *Pharaoh*.

(Joshua 2:8-11) In the future Messianic kingdom, God will be known by the whole world. **(Zechariah 14:9)**

In the case of *Pharaoh* after he ⋆ *hardened his own heart,* God chose to *harden his heart* even deeper and use him for His glory. **(Study Exo. 7:13, 7:22, 8:15, 8:19, 8:32, 9:7,** and **9:34)** Again, this stands to be repeated because of so many who have misrepresented the text; Paul is not referring to Pharaoh's eternal damnation. While we should not expect to see Pharaoh in the future kingdom, the point is that God showed *mercy to Moses,* and He ⋆ chose to *harden the heart of Pharaoh* for His purpose.

⋆ *(God chose to use pagan nations like the Assyrians, the Babylonians, the Greeks, and the Romans to punish Israel for its idolatrous ways. Paul was writing to the Roman believers in Christ just a few short years from the time when God would use Rome to destroy the Jewish Temple in Jerusalem in 70AD. Paul is reminding his Roman readers that God is having mercy on them, and He is also hardening the Jews who have chosen not to believe in Jesus. Unbelieving Israel started the unbelieving process, and God is confirming it.* **(Romans 11:25)** *We should be reminded in this fallen, evil world in which we live that God is in control of everything, and He will use evil dictators and nations for His purpose. The finite mind cannot penetrate into the infinite counsels of Almighty God.)*

> **Romans 9:19-21 -** ***Thou wilt say then unto me, Why doth he yet find fault? For who hath resisted his will? Nay but, O man, who art thou that repliest against God? Shall the thing formed say to him that formed it, Why hast thou made me thus? Hath not the potter power over the clay, of the same***

lump to make one vessel unto honour, and another unto dishonour?

From a human standpoint if God hardens hearts, then how can He blame someone for the evil he is doing or for his unbelief? Paul is dealing with the attitude of the human heart that would even think to ask this question. Paul uses the illustration of a *potter having control over the clay.* The potter can make the vessel a very simple-looking piece of pottery *(dishonor),* or a very expensive porcelain dish *(honor).* The point is that God declared that man is responsible for believing in Christ or not believing in Christ. It is God that designed the plan of salvation before the world was ever created. People are not condemned because God hardens them, but because they love darkness rather than light. **(John 3:18-19)** *"There is none righteous, no, not one."* **(Romans 3:10)** It is absurd for a sinful creature to question the Creator God as being unrighteous just because He shows *honor* to a person who reflects His glory, and He shows *dishonor* to someone who does not. Sinful man is ⋆ limited on his knowledge of the Eternal God. The illustration of Pharaoh indicated that Pharaoh got what he had coming to him.

⋆ *(God knows if an individual <u>will</u> one day come to faith in Christ, and He preserves that person even through their sinful ways until the time of conversion. God knows when a person <u>will not</u> come to faith in Christ and will harden his heart and even use him for His purpose. We do not have this kind of knowledge, and we should not pre-judge anyone because of his past mistakes. It is God who is dealing with mankind accordingly!)*

God Has the Right to Glorify Himself

> **Romans 9:22-24 - *What if God, willing to shew his wrath, and to make his power known, endured with much longsuffering the vessels of wrath fitted to destruction: And that he might make known the riches of his glory on the vessels of mercy, which he had afore prepared unto glory, Even us, whom he hath called, not of the Jews only, but also of the Gentiles?***

A holy and righteous God has the right to glorify Himself through letting people go their own way and then receive their due punishment. Notice that the *vessels of wrath* were shown God's *longsuffering* before the wrath of God was shown to them. The Greek word *katartizo* is used here for the words *fitted to destruction.* The unbelievers *prepared themselves* for destruction even though God *endured with much longsuffering.* How can anyone murmur or complain about God after He has shown such mercy to mankind. The only reason why He has not already destroyed the planet is because He desires for *all* men to come to repentance. **(2 Peter 3:9)** The world is filled with lost people who are going about living a life of selfishness and debauchery, and yet God's love is showing them His patience and longsuffering. There are *vessels of mercy* among the *Jews and the* ★ *Gentiles.*

★ *(The Jews had been taught that Gentiles could not become vessels of honor, and that only the Jews would inherit the kingdom. It helps to remember that Paul is writing to Jewish and Gentile believers in Christ, wanting them to realize that God is pouring out His wrath on the unbelieving Jews and giving mercy to those Gentiles who will believe in Christ. It was a new concept for the Jews to hear these words. The prophets of old foretold that Gentiles would be connected to the coming Messiah of Israel:*

- ***By salvation in this present age***
- ***With the believing Jews constituting the Church***
- ***By the Messiah reigning over the Gentiles in the kingdom-age***

(Please study - Luke 2:32, Acts 13:47-48, Isaiah 11:10, Romans 15:12, Romans 11:17-24, Ephesians 2:11-12, Zechariah 12:8, Ephesians 1:23, 3:6.)

"afore prepared unto glory, Even us, whom he hath called" **-** God *prepared beforehand,* or the Greek *proetoimazo,* that everyone, Jew or Gentile, *whom he hath called*, or the Greek *kaleo, summons or invites,* who in turn *receives* Jesus Christ, God has *prepared them unto glory.* Those who receive Jesus are *the called*! Paul uses the words, *Even us,* to include himself as a Jewish believer in Christ as being part of the brethren of the Jewish/Gentile community in Rome.

> **Romans 9:25-26 -** ***As he saith also in Osee, I will call them my people, which were not my people; and her beloved, which was not beloved. And it shall come to pass, that in the place where it was said unto them, Ye are not my people; there shall they be called the children of the living God.***

Although the majority of Israel is still in unbelief, God is using this time or dispensation to call Gentiles into the kingdom. This is not necessarily a fulfillment of **Hosea 2:23,** but it parallels the 8th century BC situation in the prophet ⋆ *Hosea's* day of God dealing with the idolatrous northern kingdom of Israel. The Jews in the northern kingdom *(the ten tribes)*, under the wicked king Rehoboam, would be temporarily expelled from the Land of Israel but later would repent and become God's people again. They moved from being *not my people to my people.* In Paul's day God was calling Gentiles, who in the Jewish mind *were not a people,* but now those who believed in Christ were being called *the children of the living God.*

★ *(It is interesting that the name "Hosea," which means "salvation," comes from* **Numbers 13:16,** *where God had Moses to change his name to Yehoshua, or later shortened to be Yahshua, the Hebrew name of Jesus. God extended His mercy to the Gentiles through His Son Jesus, who is the Only One who can bring salvation.)*

> **Romans 9:27-29 -** ***Esaias also crieth concerning Israel, Though the number of the children of Israel be as the sand of the sea, a remnant shall be saved: For he will finish the work, and cut it short in righteousness: because a short work will the Lord make upon the earth. And as Esaias said before, Except the Lord of Sabaoth had left us a seed, we had been as Sodoma, and been made like unto Gomorrha.***

The rejection of Israel was all part of God's purpose in giving the ★ Gentiles an opportunity to be saved. While Israel as a nation is in unbelief, there is a *remnant* of the Jews who will come to Jesus as its Messiah and *shall be saved.* God's Word will not fail and is presently being fulfilled. Paul is quoting from the prophet **Isaiah 1:9, 10:22-23.** Just like the destruction of ★★ *Sodom and Gomorrah,* if God did not have a *remnant* of Israel who trusted in Jesus, the entire nation would be destroyed. God is keeping the nation of Israel alive through the believing remnant.

★ *(This was prophesied in places like* **Isaiah 49:1-13,** *where even though Israel would go through a time of being scattered and in unbelief, God would send a light to the Gentiles.)*

★★ *(In* **Genesis 18:32,** *Abraham pleaded with God not to destroy Sodom and Gomorrah if there were only ten righteous people, but there were only Lot and his small family. There were not enough righteous people to keep the cities from being totally destroyed. Israel as a nation would be preserved because God has left a seed that does believe in Jesus. There was a remnant looking for the Messiah when Jesus came the first time, such as Zacharias, Elizabeth, Simeon, Mary, Joseph, etc. There will be a remnant of the nation of Israel saved when Jesus returns the second time,* **Zechariah 13:9.** *This truth is overlooked by many today in regard to God's plan for national Israel. During the Great Tribulation, the time called Jacob's (Israel's) Trouble,* **Jeremiah 30:7,** *only a remnant will be delivered.* **Matthew 24:22.***)*

> **Romans 9:30-31 - *What shall we say then? That the Gentiles, which followed not after righteousness, have attained to righteousness, even the righteousness which is of faith. But Israel, which followed after the law of righteousness, hath not attained to the law of righteousness.***

Here we find again the strange paradox. Even though the Gentiles were not pursuing *righteousness*, God's mercy overtook them by the gospel, and they received it through *faith.* There may have been *some* Gentiles who were seeking for the one true God, but as a general rule, they did not diligently seek *righteousness.* The reason why Israel as a nation did not *attain righteousness* is because it was seeking it through the *Law*, or by works. Though Israel was pursuing a legal righteousness with zeal, it was *out of its reach.*

> **Romans 9:32-33 - *Wherefore? Because they sought it not by faith, but as it were by the works of the law. For they stumbled at that stumblingstone; As it is written, Behold, I lay in Sion a stumblingstone and rock of offence: and whosoever believeth on him shall not be ashamed.***

The responsibility was laid on Israel for not having faith in Jesus as its Messiah. While God had chosen the nation of Israel to be a special people to take the message of Christ to the world, the nation had failed in the plan. Just because they were a chosen people did not excuse them from believing in Jesus.

Paul mentions the words of **Isaiah 8:14** and **28:16.** The fact that Jesus became a stumbling stone to the nation of Israel is mentioned by Jesus in **Matthew 21:43-44,** mentioned by Paul in **Romans 9:32-33, I Cor. 1:23,** and by the Apostle Peter in **I Peter 2:1-10.** The Greek verb *proskopto* carries a deeper meaning than *stumbling*, but rather *"to cause to strike against something."* The crucified Jesus *collided* with Israel's preconceived ideas of its Messiah. Even though it was all in God's plan, Jesus died a violent death by His own brethren.

CHAPTER TEN

The Ignorance of Israel

> **Romans 10:1-3 -** ***Brethren, my heart's desire and prayer to God for Israel is, that they might be saved. For I bear them record that they have a zeal of God, but not according to knowledge. For they being ignorant of God's righteousness, and going about to establish their own righteousness, have not submitted themselves unto the righteousness of God.***

Notice that Paul uses the term *"Brethren,"* uniting all believers with himself. Why would *Paul pray so fervently for Israel to be saved* if it was already predestined who is going to be saved or lost? The word for *"Israel"* here is *"auton,"* which means "them or they," and is the third person pronoun for the *Jews*. Paul is continuing his thought from the previous chapter regarding the unbelief of Israel, and he did not want the Gentile believers in Rome to think that he had hostility toward the unbelieving Jews. Paul not only is concerned, he is pouring his heart out to God that they might be *saved*, or the Greek *soteria*, or *delivered*. The unbelieving, religious Jews had *zeal* for

God but without knowledge as Paul had known in his previous life before meeting Jesus on the Damascus Road. Sincerity, religion, and zeal are not sufficient for salvation. They did not know God through *Yeshua*/Jesus being their Messiah. Notice the same point was made in the prophet Hosea's time:

***My people are destroyed for lack of knowledge:* Hosea 4:6a**

The unbelieving nation of Israel was and still is ignorant in two ways:

★ ***Salvation is by faith in Jesus the Messiah***

★ ***Righteousness cannot be attained by the Law***

One of the common questions asked is, ***"Why does Israel not believe in Jesus as their Messiah?"*** The unbelieving Jew is trying to *establish his own righteousness* through interpreting the Mosaic Law through the ★ *Talmud*, which includes the *Mishnah* and rabbinical Judaism.

★ *(What started as the oral teachings of the rabbis and outward ceremonialism, before and during Jesus' time, became an increasingly complex collection of interpretations, opinions, and debates that were compiled around 200AD, called the Mishnah. Over the next few centuries the Talmud became the centerpiece of religious Jews. Since the Temple was destroyed in 70AD, rabbinical Judaism has given the religious Jews a binding structure that keeps them together as a people. This misguided zeal is a major part of the blindness of the religious Jews until this day. We also need to remember that over 50 percent of the Jews in the world are not religious; they are secular Jews.)*

To parallel this thought, there are many professing Christians today who have a zeal for their denomination, or their brand of *"church,"* while still living in *ignorance* to the finished work of Jesus Christ.

> **Romans 10:4-5 - *For Christ is the end of the law for righteousness to every one that believeth. For Moses describeth the righteousness which is of the law, That the man which doeth those things shall live by them.***

The Law has not come to an *end* in the sense of no longer reflecting God's holy standard or no longer showing us our need for a Savior, but the Law is no longer the basis for our relationship with God; it is our faith in Christ! The *end*, or *telos*, of the Law can mean *"termination or goal."* The Lord Jesus Christ was the real intent and *goal* of the Law. The blood of Christ brought in the New Covenant and did what the Law of Moses could not do:

> ***In that he saith, A new covenant, he hath made the first old. Now that which decayeth and waxeth old is ready to vanish away.* Hebrews 8:13**

Israel had failed to realize that the Law had ended as a rule of salvation and the rule of life. After someone is born again, the rule of life is the *Law of Christ.* **(Galatians 6:2, Matthew 5-7)** Paul is referring to **Leviticus 18:5** when he mentions that Moses wrote about a *righteousness and life* that could only be attained if the people would *do what was written in the Law* perfectly and completely, which was not possible. Notice this parallels with what Jesus told a religious leader who thought that he could *do something* to attain eternal life:

> ***And, behold, a certain lawyer stood up, and tempted him, saying, Master, what shall I do to inherit eternal life? He said unto him, What is written in the law? how readest thou? And he answering said, Thou shalt love the Lord thy God with all thy heart, and with all thy soul, and with all thy strength, and with all thy mind; and thy neighbour as thyself. And he said unto him, Thou hast answered right: this do, and thou shalt live.*** **Luke 10:25-28**

Israel's zeal was so bent on *doing* what was written in the Law that it stumbled over having *faith* in Jesus, which it could not *do*. Gaining *life* through the Law was impossible, and Israel needed to experience the *new life in Christ;* this was Paul's heartfelt desire for it.

> **Romans 10:6-8 -** ***But the righteousness which is of faith speaketh on this wise, Say not in thine heart, Who shall ascend into heaven? (that is, to bring Christ down from above:) Or, Who shall descend into the deep? (that is, to bring up Christ again from the dead.) But what saith it? The word is nigh thee, even in thy mouth, and in thy heart: that is, the word of faith, which we preach;***

Paul is drawing a sharp contrast between the righteousness which is by the Law as spoken through Moses, and *the righteousness which is by faith* in Christ that Paul is proclaiming. Paul is using a collage of scriptural phrases to present his case. Compare these Old Testament verses:

It is not in heaven, that thou shouldest say, Who shall go up for us to heaven, and bring it unto us, that we may hear it, and do it? Neither is it beyond the sea, that thou shouldest say, Who shall go over the sea for us, and bring it unto us, that we may hear it, and do it? But the word is very nigh unto thee, in thy mouth, and in thy heart, that thou mayest do it. **Deuteronomy 30:12-14**

There were three streams of Jewish thought that Paul was alluding to here. The first was that if the Jews would keep the Law perfectly, then the Messiah (Jesus) would come down. The second thought was that if Jesus is the Christ, then He died and is still in the grave. The third was that the Messiah had not yet come. Notice that Paul mentions the *heart* twice in these verses because Israel's heart was the primary problem, and faith-based righteousness is *near.* One does not need to *ascend to heaven or descend to hell* to get to Christ. Jesus has already come down from *heaven* and has already gone ⋆ down into the *deep,* or *abyss,* and come forth. True righteousness can be attained through faith that is as near as their own *hearts and mouths.* This was the gospel that Paul and the other Apostles were *preaching.*

⋆ ***(Now that he ascended, what is it but that he also descended first into the lower parts of the earth? He that descended is the same also that ascended up far above all heavens, that he might fill all things.)*** **Ephesians 4:9-10**

Romans 10:9-10 - ***That if thou shalt confess with thy mouth the Lord Jesus, and shalt believe in thine heart that God hath raised him from the dead, thou shalt be saved.***

For with the heart man believeth unto righteousness; and with the mouth confession is made unto salvation.

Most of the time when preachers quote these well-known verses, they never connect them to what Moses said in **Deuteronomy 30** or to the Jewish context in which Paul is writing. The righteousness of God comes through ⋆ *confessing with our mouths and believing in our hearts* the finished work of Jesus Christ! We must agree with what God has said and done through His Son, Jesus. Notice that we must confess that ⋆⋆ ***Jesus is the Lord***. He is much more than a rabbi, or great teacher, or a miracle worker. No Jew would *confess* that *Jesus is Lord*, or the Greek *kurios*, if he had not truly trusted in Christ. No Gentile would *confess* that *Jesus is Lord* if he had not ceased worshipping Caesar as god.

⋆ *(There has been much damage over the years by telling people that they must make a public confession of faith in some local church to be saved. This sounds good and noble, but this alone does not bring salvation. The confessing and believing must be done toward God! Many people are saved by reading a gospel tract, by hearing the message of Christ on TV in their home, or hearing the gospel on the radio while riding in an automobile down the road. If a public confession were required for salvation, then this would be based on works. True faith in Jesus as Lord must not be suppressed, but confessed to God. Then we will have the Spirit and the courage to confess Christ out in the world. This author used to preach on Transworld Shortwave Radio Network. Messages were sent to people who walked over 20 miles in the desert just to hear the broadcasts. God was working in their hearts, and the rest of the world did not even know it.)*

★★ *(Another false teaching that has developed is by using this phrase to teach a lordship salvation, which means that Jesus must be Master of every facet of one's life from the beginning, or he was never saved in the first place. This phrase, Jesus is Lord, is referring to the Deity of Jesus. A belief and confession must be made to God the Father that Jesus is the Lord! The name, Jesus, emphasizes His humanity, while* ***Lord*** *emphasizes His divinity. The act of making Jesus the Lord of our lives is a* <u>*process*</u> *that comes* <u>*after*</u> *we are saved.)*

Paul mentions that a person *shalt believe in the heart that God hath raised him from the dead,* encompassing the entire finished work of Christ. **(I Cor. 15:3-4)** We must leave the whole matter of salvation in His hands. It is more than just believing certain truths about Jesus; it is resting on Him and depending on Him as the foundation of our hope.

Romans 10:11 - *For the scripture saith, Whosoever believeth on him shall not be ashamed.*

The word for *whosoever* is the Greek word *"pas,"* and it means *"all, every, a whole."* This again confronts the false theory that only a certain few are *predestined* to be saved. Just because the majority of Israel is still in unbelief should not discourage other Jews to believe in Jesus as their Messiah. Jesus told the religious leaders of His day that they were *responsible* for not believing in Him:

> ***O Jerusalem, Jerusalem, thou that killest the prophets, and stonest them which are sent unto thee, how often would I have gathered thy children together, even as a hen gathereth her chickens under her wings, and ye would not!*** **Matthew 23:37**

> ***And ye will not come to me, that ye might have life.* John 5:40**

Paul is quoting from two passages of scripture: **Isaiah 28:16** and **Isaiah 49:23.** Since Paul is quoting from the Old Testament, we need to look at the Hebrew word for *"ashamed,"* which is *"bosh."* The word carries a wide definition depending on how it is used. In this context everyone who believes in Jesus *will not delay, he will hurry* to confess Him. *Believing and confessing* are connected together. It can also mean that everyone who *confesses* Jesus will not be *embarrassed.* People who are truly saved will continue to confess Christ; it is not just a one-time event.

> **Romans 10:12-13 - *For there is no difference between the *Jew and the Greek: for the same Lord over all is rich unto all that call upon him. For whosoever shall call upon the name of the Lord shall be saved.***

Before Paul's conversion as a Jewish believer in Jesus, he was persecuting *"all"* followers, **(Acts 9:14)** and now he is preaching that *the Lord over all is rich unto all that call upon him.* Again, Paul is using the word *whosoever,* but this time from a different Old Testament verse:

> ***And it shall come to pass, that whosoever shall call on the name of the Lord shall be delivered: for in mount Zion and in Jerusalem shall be deliverance, as the Lord hath said, and in the remnant whom the Lord shall call.* Joel 2:32**

The Lord will deliver *anyone* or *everyone* who *believes and confesses* that Jesus is Lord, whether he is a part of the *remnant or non-remnant.* The prophet Joel was referring to *national Israel,* but Paul uses this verse in this context to say that *whosoever* believes and confesses that Jesus is Lord may be *delivered.* What an affront this *simple truth* is for any Jew who may think that he can be saved by trying to keep the works of the Law, or by thinking that the only way a Gentile could be saved was to be converted to Judaism. The familiarity of **Romans 10:9-13** can give us a presupposition that we already know something, though we have never grasped the magnitude of what Paul is saying.

This also again helps to explain the complicated words like *election* from **Romans 9,** or *predestined* from **Romans 8.** In summary, the invitation of the gospel goes out to everyone! God *predestined* that all who believe *in Jesus* will one day be made *like Jesus.* God *elected* the nation of Israel for the Savior to come through. Just because Israel is a chosen nation does not exempt its people from having to *believe and confess in Jesus as Lord* in order to be saved. Jews do not stop being Jews, and Gentiles do not stop being Gentiles. Everyone who believes in Jesus is part of the true Church. How God deals with national Israel is another subject that Paul addresses in the following chapter.

★ *(There are some 650 ethnic groups in about 195 countries in the world. Being saved is not a matter of being born a Jew or being born into the right family as a Gentile. Sinful human beings have always boasted about their family heritage of genealogy. In this context Paul is letting the Jews in Rome know that when it comes to salvation, God loves the Gentiles of the world as much as He does the Jew. Jesus is Lord of the Jews, and He is Lord of the Gentiles. Salvation's offer is universal! Christ died for all.* **John 3:16, I John 2:2***)*

ISRAEL'S IGNORANCE OF THE PREACHING OF THE GOSPEL

> **Romans 10:14-15 - *How then shall they call on him in whom they have not believed? and how shall they believe in him of whom they have not heard? and how shall they hear without a preacher? And how shall they preach, except they be sent? as it is written, How beautiful are the feet of them that preach the gospel of peace, and bring glad tidings of good things!***

The gospel of Christ being available to everyone necessitates the *preaching of the gospel* to all. It is not God's fault that Israel does not believe in Christ, because the gospel has been preached since Jesus' time. Israel has heard the gospel, and it still remains stubborn and rebellious. Paul wanted the Jewish believers in Rome to keep trying to reach their Jewish families, and the fact that God was giving the Gentiles a chance to be saved was foretold in the Old Testament scriptures. One of the key points that Paul brings out is that Israel's unbelief and ignorance regarding the righteousness available through faith in Christ has led to the universal preaching of the gospel around the world.

Notice there is a chain of four questions that Paul gives here that forms the basis for the next question:

- ***There is no calling upon the Lord without faith***
- ***There can be no faith without hearing the gospel***
- ***There is no hearing without preaching***
- ***There is no preacher unless he is sent by God***

A true preacher of the gospel must be sent or called by God. A preacher of the gospel is not someone who just chose to go into the ministry as an occupation or because he is following what others have been doing. A true preacher of the gospel is not driven by pride, money, or popularity. God could have chosen any means for giving the message of salvation to all, such as angelic messengers or directly working without a preacher. God's *"normal"* way of bringing people to Jesus Christ is through the preaching of the gospel. That does not necessarily mean that a person has to be standing behind a pulpit; he can be preaching anywhere and by many different means. Sometimes the message of Christ is preached by reading and explaining the Bible. Sometimes the message of Christ may come through a personal verbal witness to an individual. Sometimes the message of Christ is clear enough in a song to draw people to Jesus.

"as it is written, How beautiful are the feet of them that * preach the gospel of peace, and bring glad tidings of good things!" - This comes from **Isaiah 52:7,** which is a very profound connection. Isaiah is referring to the time that restores Zion and how is He going to do that. One way is by the preaching of the gospel! Again, we must see the Jewish backdrop to what Paul is saying. The reason why the feet of those who are sent to preach the gospel are *beautiful* is because they are partnering with God for the salvation of men. The feet speak of moving about from place to place and are active in preaching the gospel. Obviously, the salvation that Isaiah wrote about and that Paul is preaching about is not by the works of the Law. The *glad tidings of good things, the gospel of peace,* is that sinners can be made right with God through faith in what Christ has done for them, not in trying to work and be good enough.

⋆ *(To preach the Word of God is communicating to the people what God had already given in His written Word. Many times what people think is "preaching" is no more than religious clichés, a platitude, or stories. People are more impressed by academic discussion or scholarly interpretations than they are about hearing God's Word. The world needs less expounding and less opinions and more of "preaching God's Word." It is the preached Word that draws people to salvation!)*

> **Romans 10:16-17 - *But they have not all obeyed the gospel. For Esaias saith, Lord, who hath believed our report? So then faith cometh by hearing, and hearing by the word of God.***

The prophet Isaiah even prophesied that most of Israel would not believe the gospel. **(Isaiah 53:1)** The Greek word for *obeyed* is *hupakouo,* and it means *"to listen, or to answer."* Israel has refused to listen to the gospel, and therefore it did not *answer* the gospel. People only believe when they have a message to believe in. To have the faith in Christ to be saved, one needs to ⋆ *hear the Word of God.* This is why we must be busy about preaching God's Word, because God uses the preached Word to stir up faith in the heart of the listener. How do we increase our faith after we have received Jesus? It is done by studying God's Word and getting under the sound of the Word. It helps to be around Bible-believing people who want to talk about God's Word.

⋆ *(The average first-century person, Jew or Gentile, could not read, or read very poorly. They needed to hear the gospel preached. The sense of hearing is a God-given sense that allows us to hear the precious message of Jesus, and our faith in Christ makes the Word we have heard come alive in our hearts. The Greek "rhema" is used for "word of God" in* **Romans 10:17.** *Normally, the word "logos" is used, but the word "rhema" is referring to God's Word that has been spoken.)*

Israel is Without Excuse

> **Romans 10:18 - *But I say, Have they not heard? Yes verily, their sound went into all the earth, and their words unto the * ends of the world.***

Referring to **Psalm 19:4,** the message came even through nature itself *into all the earth.* How? Even creation itself should have brought the Jews to salvation, like the pagan Gentiles. **(Romans 1:20)** The Jews of the first century had more than the witness of nature, *(a general revelation)*; they had the very Son of God in their midst, and then the preaching of the gospel of the Risen Lord, *(a special revelation)* They still refused the message. The problem was not that Israel had not heard the message, the problem was it rejected the message of Christ.

* *(By the time of Paul's writing the gospel had already been heard unto the ends of the world, or at least farther than the Roman Empire. The Apostles of Jesus had gone as far as India, and no doubt Paul was aware of their work.)*

> **Romans 10:19 - *But I say, Did not Israel know? First Moses saith, I will provoke you to jealousy by them that are no people, and by a foolish nation I will anger you.***

This is an amazing truth that was even stated by Moses in **Deut. 32:21.** The Hebrew Bible clearly predicted a period of time when salvation would be sent out to the Gentiles, and this would cause a point of jealousy between Jews and Gentiles. Today the *"Church,"* made up of believing Jews and Gentiles from all nationalities, is this entity, or *by them that are no people;* has *provoked the unbelieving Jews to ★ jealousy.* Israel is now more accountable because Moses and Paul wrote about this jealousy, trying to stir it to believe in Jesus. Interesting!

★ *(Once this author was teaching in the Land of Israel and the Jewish guide, who was a believer in Jesus, began to weep. She stated, "I love the Messiah, but I do not love Him as much as you do; you provoke me to jealousy!" The Israeli government in the Knesset is trying to pass a bill where the gospel cannot be shared with any adult in Israel without being sent to prison for a year, and two years if shared with a child. If and when this bill passes, it will definitely affect the Christians who are traveling to Israel and the estimated 30,000 professing Jewish Christians now living in Israel. Sometimes we forget that the scribes and Pharisees were <u>envious</u> of Jesus.* **Matthew 27:18***)*

> **Romans 10:20-21 - *But Esaias is very bold, and saith, I was found of them that sought me not; I was made manifest unto them that asked not after me. But to Israel he saith, All day long I have stretched forth my hands unto a disobedient and gainsaying people.***

As strange as it may seem, it too was foretold in **Isaiah 65:1** that Israel would reject its own Messiah, while He would be *manifested unto them that asked not after me (Gentiles).* Then Paul quotes **Isaiah 65:2** when Israel rejected

Jesus as its Messiah, it was essentially rejecting the God of Israel. God has an attitude of Divine love by *stretching forth His hands to them.* In spite of the nation of Israel rejecting Christ as a whole, more and more Jews are coming to faith in Jesus, as well as more Gentile believers. God's ★ wedding banquet will be filled with people from all over the world who will one day be in heaven.

★ *(Jesus gave the Parable of the Wedding Guests in* **Matthew 22:1-14.** *The meaning was a King made ready a wedding feast and first sent out invitations to the remnant, referring to Israel. The remnant slew many of the servants, and the King was wroth and burned down the city (Jerusalem). The King sent forth more servants into the highways (Gentiles) and they gathered the bad and the good to the wedding. The result was that the wedding was furnished with guests. One came into the wedding without wearing a wedding garment (sign of righteousness) and he was cast into outer darkness. Jesus closed the parable by saying, "Many are called, but few are chosen." The* <u>*called*</u> *was Israel first, but it rejected the call, then the called were the Gentiles, and many accepted the invitation. The* <u>*chosen*</u> *were the ones who accepted the invitation. God's heaven will be filled with people from all nations, kindreds,* and tongues that will be clothed in righteousness. **Revelation 7:9***)*

CHAPTER ELEVEN

RESTORATION OF ISRAEL

Romans 11:1 - *I say then, Hath God cast away his people? God forbid. For I also am an Israelite, of the seed of Abraham, of the tribe of Benjamin.*

After presenting Israel's rejection of its Messiah, Paul raises a question that has baffled believers for centuries. If God the Father sent Jesus into the world in the *fullness of time,* knowing *when* the nation would reject Jesus as its Messiah, and yet Israel was responsible for its own choices, does this mean that *God has cast away His people?* The Greek word for *"cast away"* is *"apotheo,"* and it means *"to push away, or to refuse."* Paul answers again using the Hebrew idiom, *chalilah,* or *"far be it"* translated, *"God forbid!"* What about all the promises that God made to *national Israel?* ★ Do those promises now belong to the New Testament Church, as many denominations are teaching today? How do we connect the dots with what Paul has already said in the previous chapter? The believing Jews are part of the New Testament Church, **(Gal. 3:28, Col. 3:11)** but what about the *nation, the Holy Land,* and the fact that Jesus said that He was coming back to

Israel when He returns? (**Zechariah 14:4, Matthew 19:28, Matthew 23:39)** The fact that most of Israel has rejected Jesus, it does not mean that He has rejected Israel. Many people refuse to accept biblical truth when it does not make practical sense. Israel is still the chosen people of God no matter what anyone may think or teach.

★ *(The theory or idea of a new Israel that is largely made up of Gentile believers is not taught in the Sacred Scriptures. Paul is teaching here about the physical nation of Israel that goes by that name.)*

"For I also am an Israelite, of the seed of Abraham, of the tribe of Benjamin" - The first proof that God has not cast away His people is that the one who is writing this epistle is an Israelite! Unlike some people in our world today who think or say they are Jews and are not, Paul knew that he was *of the seed of Abraham, of the tribe of* ★ *Benjamin.* The fact that Paul's faith was in Jesus the Messiah proved there were some Jews who had embraced the gospel. Even after he accepted Jesus and became His follower, Paul was still identified as being from *the tribe of Benjamin.* He was still a Jew!

★ *(No doubt that Saul, later named Paul, was named after king Saul in the Old Testament, who also was from the tribe of Benjamin.* **I Samuel 9:21***)*

Romans 11:2a - *God hath not cast away his people which he foreknew.*

Paul is not referring to some *hidden foreknowledge/predestination* of individual Jews here, he is referring to the *foreknowledge of the nation of Israel* that would bless the world through which would come Jesus the Messiah-the Son of

God! God knew that Israel would reject Christ, and then the Gentiles would have a chance to hear the gospel. God has a covenantal relationship with His chosen people. As we will see later in this chapter, this does not mean that *ALL* of the Jews will be saved in the end as some extreme Zionists believe, but God has a plan and a purpose for the nation of Israel.

★ *(The title Zionists comes from the hill in Jerusalem, called Tzion, that appears over 150 times in the Bible. In* **2 Samuel 5:6-9,** *it was the Jebusite city that was captured by king David in the 10th century BC and established as his royal capital. The modern-day Zionist movement, started in 1897 by Theodore Herzl in Europe, helped to re-establish the nation of Israel in 1948. The Zionistic view has been a thought of many Jews since the Temple was destroyed in 70AD.)*

> **Romans 11:2b-4 -** ***Wot ye not what the scripture saith of Elias? how he maketh intercession to God against Israel saying, Lord, they have killed thy prophets, and digged down thine altars; and I am left alone, and they seek my life. But what saith the answer of God unto him? I have reserved to myself seven thousand men, who have not bowed the knee to the image of Baal.***

Paul wanted the believers in Rome to know that the unbelief within national Israel has been a long-running problem. Israel has always been a disobedient people, but there have always been some who walked with the Lord, and they are called *the remnant,* or *of Israel.* **(Romans 2:29, 9:6)** Paul uses the story of *Elias*, or *Elijah*, in **I Kings 19.** Elijah thought that he was the only believer in the God of Israel who was left and *even prayed against his own people.* God showed Elijah that he was not alone, and there were *seven thousand* believers that he did not even ★ know about *who had not bowed the knee to the image of Baal.* While *seven thousand* in an entire nation may not seem a lot, it was enough to prove Paul's point. While apostasy was general, it was not universal among the Jews.

★ *(This is the only time in Paul's writings that he refers to the book of I Kings. Paul wanted his readers to know that as godly as the prophet Elijah was, he was wrong about all of the Israelites being in unbelief. God's purpose and plan for the nation of Israel was still on course in spite of the apostasy. While still being a minority, there were probably more believers in the tribe of Judah during Elijah's time. There are more Jewish believers in Christ today than the world knows about. Several hundred thousand are listed as Messianic Jews, and over 300 congregations in the US and Israel. Almost every nation has at least one or more Messianic congregations.)*

Romans 11:5 - *Even so then at this present time also there is a remnant according to the election of grace.*

The Greek word for *"election"* here is *"ekloge,"* or *"choice, selection, (divine)."* This word does not mean the same thing that ★ *"election"* does in an English theological discourse. God had kept for Himself *a remnant* that responded to His grace in Christ. We often think that God needs a lot of people to do His great work, but it only takes a ★★ small group. The believing Jews, or the *remnant according to the election of grace*, were a small group in Paul's day, but they continued in the first century and still exist today. While the number of the believers in Rome were mostly

Gentiles, it was started by the believing Jews **(Acts 2:5-11)** and was far from being *exclusively* Gentile.

* *(In English theology the word "election" means that God "elected" who would and who would not be saved before the world began. This definition does not reconcile with many other scriptures. Again, when the inspired Word of God explains away our interpretation of a verse, a word, or a phrase, then our interpretation must be incorrect. In the Holy Bible, the word "elect" or "election" can refer to the "Messiah, mine elect" in* **Isaiah 42:1**, *or the "elect" angels in* **I Timothy 5:21**, *or Israel is called the "elect" in* **Isaiah 45:4**, *or the Jews or Gentiles who accepted Christ were called the "elect." God also "elects" certain individuals like the Apostles in* **John 15:16** *in the first century to carry the gospel for the very first time into the known world. God "elected" Paul to take the gospel to the Gentiles. God still "elects" individuals to do a special work and gives them their own particular gifts for His purpose. The Bible is clear that God desired for ALL to be saved. We must understand the difference between salvation and service.* **Romans 9:11** *is referring to the election of national Israel and the remnant who had accepted Jesus as their Messiah.)*

** *(The kingdom of God started with Jesus and His disciples in the Galilee. Like the mustard seed and the leaven in the kingdom parables,* **Matthew 13:32-33**, *what started out so small would eventually affect the whole world.)*

> **Romans 11:6 -** ***And if by grace, then is it no more of works: otherwise grace is no more grace. But if it be of works, then it is no more grace: otherwise work is no more work.***

How does the remnant of the Jews come to faith in Jesus as its Messiah? *By God's grace!* As Paul has stated repeatedly in this epistle, the Jews or Gentiles cannot be saved by their *works*, trying to keep the Law, or a combination of the two. To add *works* to God's *grace* would destroy the character of both. The Jews who had responded to the gospel of Christ were saved totally *by grace* and were not predicated on their morality or because they were superior to other Jews.

> **Romans 11:7-8 -** ***What then? Israel hath not obtained that which he seeketh for; but the election hath obtained it, and the rest were blinded. (According as it is written, God hath given them the spirit of slumber, eyes that they should not see, and ears that they should not hear;) unto this day.***

The reason why God has hardened the unbelieving Jew is because he was, and still is *unto this day* trying to *seek* the impossible; acceptance before a holy God through the works of the Law. Not only have they not received salvation through Christ, they have ⋆*frustrated* God's grace and caused a spiritual blindness. *The spirit of slumber and eyes that they should not see, and ears that they should not hear* are alluding to ⋆⋆ **Isaiah 6:9-10** and **Isaiah 29:10**, and our Lord Jesus even used it in **John 12:40** when talking to the unbelieving Jews of His day.

⋆ *("I do not frustrate the grace of God: for if righteousness come by the law, then Christ is dead in vain".)* **Galatians 2:21**

⋆⋆ *(The blindness of Israel is such an important part of the gospel going to the Gentiles that this thought is further extended in* **Matthew 13:14-15** *and* **Acts 28:26-27.** *We must remember that the blindness of Israel is not final, as we will we see in the latter part of this chapter.)*

> **Romans 11:9-10** - ***And David saith, Let their table be made a snare, and a trap, and a stumblingblock, and a recompence unto them: Let their eyes be darkened, that they may not see, and bow down their back alway.***

It is astonishing how the Sacred Scriptures are like a beautiful piece of divine tapestry: woven with the inspiration of the Holy Spirit. Paul is now using the testimony of David **(Psalm 69:22-23).** The blessings of Israel were like provisions set out on the *table, but they became a snare and a trap.* Israel's blessing had turned into a source of Jewish pride and lured the people into seeking righteousness by means of the Law. Since Paul is using **Psalm 69:22-23** for his reference, we need to look at the original Hebrew thought. The Hebrew wording in the Psalms is *"loins,"* or *"mothen"* which means *"waist or hips."* Paul is using the Greek word *"noton,"* translated *"back."* Not only are *their eyes darkened,* but they are also *bent over by the weight of the load* of trying to keep the works of the Law. The nation labors under the burden like a slave who is continually carrying a heavy load.

Israel's Rejection of the Messiah is Not Final

> **Romans 11:11-12** - ***I say then, Have they stumbled that they should fall? God forbid: but rather through their fall salvation is come unto the Gentiles, for to provoke them to jealousy. Now if the fall of them be the riches of the world, and the diminishing of them the riches of the Gentiles; how much more their fulness?***

Paul is repeatedly addressing a potential misunderstanding that his readers might draw from what he has previously said.

Because the nation of Israel has *stumbled*, does that mean it will ultimately be cast away? Paul uses again the Hebrew idiom, *chalilah*, or translated *"God forbid,"* that he uses some ten times throughout this epistle. Notice the difference here between *stumbling* and *fall*. The first Greek word for *fall* is *pipto*, (condemnation) while the second word for *fall* here is *paraptoma*, (trespass). Israel's sin of rejecting Christ as its Messiah would not lead to its irretrievable spiritual ruin. ⋆ God's plan is that He would use the transgression of Israel so *that salvation would come unto the Gentiles*. And again, Paul alludes to **Deut. 32:21** when talking about the salvation of the Gentiles *would provoke Israel to jealousy*. The Hebrew word in Deuteronomy is *qanah*, and it simply means *"jealous or envy,"* while the Greek word *para zeloo*, means *"I will make jealous."* This Greek word is where we get the English word *"zeal."* The idea is that the Gentile believers will come alongside the unbelieving Jews and be witnesses to them. Gentiles must never forget that the gospel only came to the world *after* the Jewish nation rejected Christ. It is not that the rejection of Israel *caused* the Gentiles to be saved, but it gave them the opportunity to be saved. Gentiles are to live the Christian life without any hatred, prejudice, persecution, or malice toward the Jewish people. It was all in God's plan. We are to live in such a way as to show them the love of Jesus!

⋆ *(God knew the exact time for Jesus to come into the world. He knew that the nation was in a dark place spiritually; it was even referred to as "the land of the shadow of death."* **(Luke 1:79)** *The All-Knowing, Almighty God of the universe would offer Israel the kingdom, knowing that it would reject Jesus as its Messiah. This would be the way that God would send the message of salvation into the known world.)*

"Now if the fall of them be the riches of the world, and the diminishing of them the riches of the Gentiles; how much more their fulness?" - Israel has been *diminished* to a remnant of believers, but this remnant has become a source of *riches for the world and for the Gentiles.* In the future, when God deals with national Israel again, the Gentiles will enjoy even a *greater blessing* than when Israel stumbled. Paul uses the Hebrew style of comparison teaching called, *kal v'chomer,* by saying, *"how much more their fullness?"* **(Study Isa. 60:1-3, 62:1-3, Mic. 4:1-4, Zech. 8:11-13, 20-23)**

> **Romans 11:13-14** - ***For I speak to you Gentiles, inasmuch as I am the apostle of the Gentiles, I magnify mine office: If by any means I may provoke to emulation them which are my flesh, and might save some of them.***

Now Paul shifts and gives a word to the *Gentile believers.* He wanted them to know that God appointed him as their *apostle*, and that he took glory in this position and calling. The Greek word for *emulation* is also *para zeloo,* the same word that is used earlier for *jealousy.* Paul wanted the Gentile believers in Rome to know that he had not washed his hands with Israel. Notice when referring to the Jews here, Paul uses the words *which are my flesh.* His prayer was the more Gentiles who embraced the gospel, the more Jews would come to saving faith in Christ. It is no accident that over the course of the centuries many of the Jewish Christians have been led to Jesus by Gentiles. However, another truth is that Gentile Christianity has provoked the Jews to wrath, rather than to jealousy.

> **Romans 11:15-16** - ***For if the casting away of them be the reconciling of the world, what shall the***

receiving of them be, but life from the dead? For if the firstfruit be holy, the lump is also holy: and if the root be holy, so are the branches.

It must be noted that this chapter has caused more confusion and more debate than any of Paul's writings. The problem lies within western-world Christianity refusing to accept or believe all of the promises that God has placed in His Word regarding Israel. Paul's statements are not anything new, but explained how **Isaiah 49** is being fulfilled to this day. Paul is using the pronoun <u>*them*</u> and different analogies referring to Israel in these two verses before he moves on to speak about the Gentiles:

- ***The rejection of Israel has resulted in the reconciling of the world***
- ***Then the acceptance of Israel will mean life from the dead***
- ***When God deals with national Israel again, it will be life from the dead***
- ***The firstfruits were the Patriarchs, like Abraham and the ancestors of the Jewish nation, who were set apart for God's purpose (The past-Old Covenant)***
- ***The lump is the small believing remnant of the Jews (The present- New Covenant)***
- ***The root is the nation of Israel that God set apart to send the Messiah through***
- ***The branches are the believing Jews who are descendants of the nation of Israel***

Paul is using the principle that God gave to Israel when its people first came into the Promised Land. The holiness of the *firstfruits* and the *root* **(Nation of Israel)** are passed on to the *lump* and the *branches* **(Believing Israel)**.

> ***And the Lord spake unto Moses, saying, Speak unto the children of Israel, and say unto them, When ye come into the land whither I bring you, Then it shall be, that, when ye eat of the bread of the land, ye shall offer up an heave offering unto the Lord. Ye shall offer up a cake of the first of your dough for an heave offering: as ye do the heave offering of the threshingfloor, so shall ye heave it. Of the first of your dough ye shall give unto the Lord an heave offering in your generations.*** **Numbers 15:17-21**

The Gentile Believers Grafted In

> **Romans 11:17-18 -** ***And if some of the branches be broken off, and thou, being a wild olive tree, wert grafted in among them, and with them partakest of the root and fatness of the olive tree; Boast not against the branches. But if thou boast, thou bearest not the root, but the root thee.***

The imagery of *some of the branches being broken off* (Unbelieving Israel) and ⋆ *grafting in a wild olive branch* (Gentile believers) is abnormal and is not the natural way they do things in the agrarian, Mesopotamian culture. One of the keys to understanding this section is the little word *"thou"* or *"you,"* which is the Greek word *"su."* Paul did not want the Gentile believers to think that Israel's present casting aside was permanent and that the Gentiles had taken Israel's place in God's plan. The *cultivated olive tree* is Israel, and the *uncultivated wild olive tree* is the Gentiles. The Gentile believers had been ⋆

grafted into the cultivated olive tree and was able to partakest in the blessings. It was not that Israel benefited from the Gentile believers, but the Gentile believers were benefiting from what flowed from Israel. It was the *root of Israel* that was *bearing* the Gentiles, not the other way around. The Gentile believers needed to have the attitude of humility and not be prideful to think that they were superior to the Jews. The false idea that the Gentile believers are the *new Israel* is preposterous and not founded in the Sacred Scriptures. Paul mentions is his epistle to the Ephesians what the blood of Christ did for the Gentile believers:

> ***Wherefore remember, that ye being in time past Gentiles in the flesh, who are called Uncircumcision by that which is called the Circumcision in the flesh made by hands; That at that time ye were without Christ, being aliens from the commonwealth of Israel, and strangers from the covenants of promise, having no hope, and without God in the world: But now in Christ Jesus ye who sometimes were far off are made nigh by the blood of Christ.*** **Ephesians 2:11-13**

* *(When an olive tree has lost its vigor and vitality, one way to remedy this was by cutting off the dead branches. It invigorates the olive tree to lose the branches that are not producing any olives. It is* <u>not normal</u> *to get a wild branch and graft it into the good olive tree. God did something unnatural when He grafted the Gentiles into the blessings of Israel. Even in the Jewish Talmud it is written that Ruth the Moabitess was a "godly shoot" engrafted into Israel.)*

> **Romans 11:19-21 -** ***Thou wilt say then, The branches were broken off, that I might be grafted in. Well; because of unbelief they were broken off, and thou standest by faith. Be not highminded, but fear: For if God spared not the natural branches, take heed lest he also spare not thee.***

This is a powerful passage where Paul even warns the Gentile believers of thinking that *God deliberately broke off some of the Jewish people so they could be grafted in.* They were *broken off* not because they were not chosen or not elected, but *because of their unbelief!* The Gentiles were not *grafted in* because of merit or good works, but because of their *faith* in the finished work of the Jewish Messiah, Jesus Christ! Wow! The Gentiles are *standing* because of the righteousness of Christ, which is by *faith.*

"Be not highminded, but fear: For if God spared not the natural branches, take heed lest he also spare not thee" **-** Paul warns the Gentiles to *be not highminded, but fear.* If they ⋆ stop responding to the gospel in faith, then God will stop dealing with them and return His focus to Israel. The Gentiles must continue in faith! This is not referring to individual salvation, but with the nationality of the Gentiles as a whole. The Gentiles are not self-sustained, but are sustained by the root: Israel and the Abrahamic Covenant.

⋆ *(At the present time the Gentile world largely rejects the gospel in the form and pattern in which the Apostle Paul preached and by the Lord Jesus Christ. They have created their own brand of Christianity and over-spiritualized the scriptures to fit their favorite doctrines. Just as Judaism in Jesus' day had degenerated into outward ceremonialism, the same thing is happening in the Gentile world by using the name*

"Christian." The time is fast approaching when this age will come to a close, and the Great Tribulation will begin. There will be 144,000 Jews who will proclaim the gospel in a new worldwide evangelistic outreach. **Matt. 24:9-14, Rev. 7:2-9, 12:17, 14:1-7**)

> **Romans 11:22-23 - *Behold therefore the goodness and severity of God: on them which fell, severity; but toward thee, goodness, if thou continue in his goodness: otherwise thou also shalt be cut off. And they also, if they abide not still in unbelief, shall be grafted in: for God is able to graft them in again.***

The Gentiles ought to think seriously about *the goodness and the severity of God.* The unbelieving Jews were experiencing *the severity of God,* and the believing Gentiles were enjoying *the goodness of God.* If the Gentiles want to continue to be a part of God's blessing, they need *to continue in God's goodness.* The Greek word for *goodness* is *chrestotes*, which is *God's kindness.* Sinful man does not have the natural ability to produce this type of kindness. The Gentiles need to continue to abide in Christ as Jesus mentioned in **John 15:1-8.** Again, not referring to a salvation of continuing but being a part of God's favor. God certainly has the full ability to *graft Israel back in again if it abides not in unbelief.*

> **Romans 11:24 - *For if thou wert cut out of the olive tree which is wild by nature, and wert grafted contrary to nature into a good olive tree: how much more shall these, which be the natural branches, be grafted into their own olive tree?***

Paul explains why the Gentiles believers in Jesus should expect Israel to be restored. The place of blessing belongs to Israel. How so? The Gentiles are sharing in the covenants that God gave to Israel. **(Romans 9:4)** Paul uses the Hebrew style of *kal v'chomer* once again when he says that the Gentiles were wild by nature, and yet God made a way for them to be *grafted in*. How much more shall God find a way to *graft in the natural branches,* or Israel, *into his own olive tree?* The purpose and plan of God for the Gentiles to be *grafted into the olive tree* is temporary. If the Gentile branches can bring forth spiritual fruit for a time, then most certainly the natural branches of Israel will bring forth spiritual fruit once the window has closed on this dispensation.

The Promise of Israel's Restoration

> **Romans 11:25 - *For I would not, brethren, that ye should be ignorant of this mystery, lest ye should be wise in your own conceits; that blindness in part is happened to Israel, until the fulness of the Gentiles be come in.***

This is one of the most significant verses in the New Testament to prove that God deals with the *Gentiles* and the nation of *Israel* in different and unique ways. The truth that this verse holds is one that needs to be preached in every local church in the world. There is so much *ignorance* in many religious circles today, and one reason is that theologians, scholars, and ministerial colleges have tried to rationalize the *mysteries of God*. When we think that we can fully comprehend the Eternal Mind of God, we become *wise in our own conceits.* God's master plan for *Israel and the Gentiles* are *unsearchable riches* and are *mysteries* that we cannot explain, and therefore we just accept them by faith. The Holy Bible gives us the simple plan of salvation so we sinners can be saved, but on the other hand, the Holy Bible contains deep and profound *mysteries* that were designed and originated within the Divine counsels of heaven. We must approach this verse asking God for His wisdom to help us not be *ignorant* and rightly divide the Word of Truth.

A New Testament *mystery* is a divine truth that was not revealed in the Hebrew Scriptures, but is revealed in the New Testament. A *mystery* is something that was *hid in God,* but was not given to the sons of men in the Old Testament. One of the great *mysteries* was that the New Testament Church, being made of believing Jews and Gentiles, was not revealed in the Old Testament. Please take the time to study these verses carefully:

> ***For this cause I Paul, the prisoner of Jesus Christ for you Gentiles, If ye have heard of the dispensation of the grace of God which is given me to you-ward: How that by revelation he made known unto me the mystery; (as I wrote afore in few words, Whereby, when ye read, ye may understand my knowledge in the mystery of Christ) Which in other ages was not made known unto the sons of men, as it is now revealed unto his holy apostles and prophets by the Spirit; That the Gentiles should be fellowheirs, and of the same body, and partakers of his promise in Christ by the gospel: Whereof I was made a minister, according to the gift of the grace of God***

> ***given unto me by the effectual working of his power. Unto me, who am less than the least of all saints, is this grace given, that I should preach among the Gentiles the unsearchable riches of Christ; And to make all men see what is the fellowship of the mystery, which from the beginning of the world hath been hid in God, who created all things by Jesus Christ:*** **Ephesians 3:1-9**

> ***Now to him that is of power to stablish you according to my gospel, and the preaching of Jesus Christ, according to the revelation of the mystery, which was kept secret since the world began, But now is made manifest, and by the scriptures of the prophets, according to the commandment of the everlasting God, made known to all nations for the obedience of faith: To God only wise, be glory through Jesus Christ for ever. Amen.*** **Romans 16:25-27**

> ***For ye see your calling, brethren, how that not many wise men after the flesh, not many mighty, not many noble, are called: But God hath chosen the foolish things of the world to confound the wise; and God hath chosen the weak things of the world to confound the things which are mighty;*** **I Corinthians 1:26-27**

"that blindness in part is happened to Israel" **-** The Greek word for *"blindness"* here is "porosis," which means *"hardening, covered over with callous."* This *blindness* is only *partial* in two ways:

- ★ ***Not all Israel (Jews) are blinded, there is a remnant that do believe in Jesus***
- ★ ***The partial blindness is only for a time, until the fullness of the Gentiles comes in***

As mentioned before, Paul did not want the Gentile believers in Rome to think that the *partial blindness to Israel* was permanent, or that the Gentiles had somehow taken Israel's place. He had already stated on several occasions that God's promises to national Israel would be fulfilled. The purpose of the *partial blindness to Israel* was so that the *fullness of the Gentiles* could come in.

"until the fulness of the Gentiles be come in" **-** The Greek word for *"fullness"* is *"pleroma,"* and it means *"completion, filling up."* Notice how this word is also used in **Matthew 23:32,** and **I Thess. 2:16.** The *partial blindness of Israel* has a limit of time; *until* the number of Gentiles that will trust in Christ is complete. ★ What does this mean? Jesus had already said that there were *other sheep* that was not within the sheepfold of Israel, and they had to be brought in. This is also what James referred to at the first Jerusalem Council:

> ***And other sheep I have, which are not of this fold: them also I must bring, and they shall hear my voice; and there shall be one fold, and one shepherd.*** **John 10:16**
>
> ***Simeon hath declared how God at the first did visit the Gentiles, to take out of them a people for his name.*** **Acts 15:14**

★ *(There is plenty of evidence in the events taking place on the world's stage today that the full harvest of the Gentiles is nearly ready. Jesus said that "Jerusalem would be trodden down of the Gentiles until the fullness of the Gentiles be fulfilled."* **(Luke 21:24)** *The city of Jerusalem was recaptured by Israel in 1967, and this is believed to be a major timeline for the fullness of the Gentiles, as far as controlling Jerusalem. Since that time, a major sweep of the Gentile harvest has taken place. When the Church Age is complete, will the catching away of the New Testament saints take place? We need to redeem the time and be ready!* **I Thess. 4:14-18***)*

As we think about the epistle Paul writing to the Romans more than 1,950 years ago, it is evident that the Gentile harvest is not yet complete. We are not seeing Gentiles come to Christ in the vast numbers of the past. The exact number of the Gentiles who will be saved is a number that is only known to God Himself. Whenever that figure is complete, God will once again turn His focus upon national Israel, not just the individual Jews.

National Israel Will Be Saved

> **Romans 11:26-27 -** ***And so all Israel shall be saved: as it is written, There shall come out of Sion the Deliverer, and shall turn away ungodliness from Jacob: For this is my covenant unto them, when I shall take away their sins.***

Paul is not quoting verbatim, but he is referring to **Isaiah 59:20-21** and **Isaiah 27:9:**

> ***And the Redeemer shall come to Zion, and unto them that turn from transgression in Jacob, saith the Lord. As for me, this is my covenant with them, saith the Lord; My spirit that is upon thee, and my words which I have put in thy mouth, shall not depart out of thy mouth, nor out of the mouth of thy seed, nor out of the mouth of thy seed's seed, saith the Lord, from henceforth and for ever.***
>
> ***By this therefore shall the iniquity of Jacob be purged; and this is all the fruit to take away his sin; when he maketh all the stones of the altar as chalkstones that are beaten in sunder, the groves and images shall not stand up.***

Israel's national salvation was not a mystery, for it was revealed in the Hebrew Scriptures. The mystery was the partial blindness of the hardening of Israel for a period of time. In some Zionist circles the phrase *"all Israel shall be saved"* has been misinterpreted to mean that all Jews of all time will eventually be saved. However, this is not what the phrase means. It refers to all of the Jews who are living at that time. Notice these verses that refer to the end of the Great Tribulation period:

> ***And it shall come to pass, that in all the land, saith the Lord, two parts therein shall be cut off and die; but the third shall be left therein. And I will bring the third part through the fire, and will refine them as silver is refined, and will try them as gold is tried: they shall call on my name, and I will hear them: I will say, It is my people: and they shall say, The Lord is my God.*** **Zechariah 13:8-9**

There were several times in the book of Exodus where the Holy Bible states that *"all Israel came out of the Egypt."* **(Exo. 12:41, 51, 13:18, 16:1, 17:1, 40:38)** Of course not all Jews who ever lived came out of Egypt, but every Jew who was living at that time. The word *"Israel"* in this verse is talking about national, ethnic Israel, just like the other ten times that Paul uses this word since **Chapter 9**. There is no reason to make an exception with the name *Israel* in this verse, when the previous verse gives the time of the Gentiles in full contrast.

The Greek word for *"Deliverer"* is *"rhuomai,"* and it means *"rescue, deliver, draw to oneself."* Jesus will return at the end of the Great Tribulation Period and plant His feet on the Mt of Olives, east of Jerusalem. The Jews who are living at that time will be delivered and look upon Him and realize that He is truly their Messiah. This will be after the horrendous seven-year period called *"Jacob's Trouble."* Notice these important verses that describe where Jesus is coming to and * what will happen to national Israel at that time:

> ***And his feet shall stand in that day upon the mount of Olives, which is before Jerusalem on the east, and the mount of Olives shall cleave in the midst thereof toward the east and toward the west, and there shall be a very great valley; and half of the mountain shall remove toward the north, and half of it toward the south.*** **Zechariah 14:4**

> ***And I will pour upon the house of David, and upon the inhabitants of Jerusalem, the spirit of grace and of supplications: and they shall look upon me whom***

> ***they have pierced, and they shall mourn for him, as one mourneth for his only son, and shall be in bitterness for him, as one that is in bitterness for his firstborn.* Zechariah 12:10**

★ *(Jesus plainly said that He will not return until the ethnic Jews acknowledge Him as their Messiah.* **(Matthew 23:39)** *When Jesus Christ returns, the entire human race will see him in judgment and wrath,* **Revelation 1:7,** *but the Jews who are alive at that time will realize that they pierced Him when He was on the earth once before. They will be saved through faith in Jesus as their Messiah. It will not be some peculiar Jewish salvation. This is when "all Israel shall be delivered" from the final wrath and sin's dominion over them.)*

"For this is my covenant unto them, when I shall take away their sins" - When we compare other scriptures with Paul's epistle in Romans, we find this covenant mentioned in **Hebrews 8:8** and **10:16**, and was brought through the blood of Christ. **(Matthew 26:28)** It is connected to the all-important promise that God gave to the prophet Jeremiah in the 6th century BC concerning His *covenant* with Israel. Please notice how powerful the words of this *covenant* to Israel really are:

> ***Behold, the days come, saith the Lord, that I will make a new covenant with the house of Israel, and with the house of Judah: Not according to the covenant that I made with their fathers in the day that I took them by the hand to bring them out of the land of Egypt; which my covenant they brake, although I was an husband unto them, saith the Lord: But this shall be the covenant that I will make with the house***

> *of Israel; After those days, saith the Lord, I will put my law in their inward parts, and write it in their hearts; and will be their God, and they shall be my people. And they shall teach no more every man his neighbour, and every man his brother, saying, Know the Lord: for they shall all know me, from the least of them unto the greatest of them, saith the Lord: for I will forgive their iniquity, and I will remember their sin no more. Thus saith the Lord, which giveth the sun for a light by day, and the ordinances of the moon and of the stars for a light by night, which divideth the sea when the waves thereof roar; The Lord of hosts is his name: If those ordinances depart from before me, saith the Lord, then the seed of Israel also shall cease from being a nation before me for ever. Thus saith the Lord; If heaven above can be measured, and the foundations of the earth searched out beneath, I will also cast off all the seed of Israel for all that they have done, saith the Lord*. **Jeremiah 31:31-37**

Notice also the *everlasting land covenant* that God made to ethnic Israel to Abraham:

> *For all the land which thou seest, to thee will I give it, and to thy seed for ever.* **Genesis 13:15**
>
> *And I will establish my covenant between me and thee and thy seed after thee in their generations for an everlasting covenant, to be a God unto thee, and to thy seed after thee. And I will give unto thee, and to thy seed after thee, the land wherein thou art a*

> ***stranger, all the land of Canaan, for an everlasting possession; and I will be their God.*** **Genesis 17:7-8**

God's Enduring Love

> **Romans 11:28-29 -** ***As concerning the gospel, they are enemies for your sakes: but as touching the election, they are beloved for the father's sakes. For the gifts and calling of God are without repentance.***

Notice the pronouns *they* and *your,* referring to Israel and the Gentiles. Even though national Israel was an *enemy* of the gospel and was against Jesus, it is still *beloved by God,* if for no other reason for the *sake of the fathers,* or the Patriarchs in the Old Testament. God made promises to them that must be fulfilled. The nature of God's promises to Israel is unconditional and unchanging. God *called* the nation of Israel to be His chosen vessel, and His promises or *gifts* to them are irrevocable. Paul connects *calling and gifts* together to emphasize the importance of God's enduring love for Israel.

> **Romans 11:30-32 -** ***For as ye in times past have not believed God, yet have now obtained mercy through their unbelief: Even so have these also now not believed, that through your mercy they also may obtain mercy. For God hath concluded them all in unbelief, that he might have mercy upon all.***

Paul gives a principle for what is going to happen concerning the calling out of the Gentiles and Israel's national salvation. Through the *unbelief* of Israel, God extended mercy to the Gentiles. If God used the disobedience of Israel for the good of the Gentiles, He can certainly show the same *mercy* to Israel in the future.

God hath *concluded*, or the Greek *sugkleio*, that *all* of the Jews and Gentiles are in need of *God's mercy.* God has caught them, so to speak, in the net of unbelief, and the only way out is by the mercy found in Jesus Christ. Notice where the same verb is used when Jesus created the multitude of fish for the disciples:

> ***And when they had this done, they inclosed*** *(sugkleio)* ***a great multitude of fishes: and their net brake.*** **Luke 5:6**

> **Romans 11:33-36 -** ***O the depth of the riches both of the wisdom and knowledge of God! how unsearchable are his judgments, and his ways past finding out! For who hath known the mind of the Lord? or who hath been his counsellor? Or who hath first given to him, and it shall be recompensed unto him again? For of him, and through him, and to him, are all things: to whom be glory for ever. Amen.***

After reflecting on God's master plan for the nation of Israel, and how God used its unbelief to show mercy to the Gentiles, Paul gives a tremendous doxology. God's *judgments* and *ways* are beyond human tracing. The concepts of *riches and wisdom and knowledge* are all parallel to each other. This verses comes to mind:

> ***For my thoughts are not your thoughts, neither are your ways my ways, saith the Lord.*** **Isaiah 55:8**

> ***Who hath directed the Spirit of the Lord, or being his counsellor hath taught him?* Isaiah 40:13**
>
> ***Who hath prevented me, that I should repay him? whatsoever is under the whole heaven is mine.* Job 41:11**

No one can give to God so much that God has to pay anyone back. Salvation comes from the Lord and it is free, so He is not in debt to anyone.

"For of him, and through him, and to him, are all things: to whom be glory for ever. Amen." **-** When we try to imagine that everything planned was not planned by man, but by the Eternal God before the world began causes us to exclaim, *glory to God forever!* Man does not have the wisdom to design such a plan, and even if he did, he would not know how to bring it to pass. Creation of the universe and then salvation was *of him,* and *through him,* and *to him.* It was all done for God's pleasure, and He alone deserves all of the praise. When we realize that God is greater than our minds can understand, that makes us worship Him all the more passionately! When this letter was read to the believers in Rome, they probably echoed out a loud reverent and solemn *Amen!*

CHAPTER TWELVE

THE FOUNDATION FOR CHRISTIAN LIVING

Romans 12:1-2 - *I beseech you therefore, brethren, by the mercies of God, that ye present your bodies a living sacrifice, holy, acceptable unto God, which is your reasonable service. And be not conformed to this world: but be ye transformed by the renewing of your mind, that ye may prove what is that good, and acceptable, and perfect, will of God.*

For the first time in this epistle Paul turns his attention on personal behavior for the believer in Christ. His primary focus has been the truths that undergird the gospel, such as the role of the Law, the place of Israel in God's unfolding purpose, and the inclusion of the Gentile believers. This is what we would call *theology*. Paul wanted the believers in Rome to know that he was not detached from how they were to live out this kingdom life. Christian living is much more than *theology*, but we can make the choice about ★ practical ways that we live for Jesus Christ in this world.

★ *(John Wesley, (1703-1791) the English theologian who founded the movement called Methodism, focused much of his preaching on the practical ways to live the Christian life. While many disagreed with Wesley's theology of the free will of man, he was highly respected as a man of God. This author has studied many of Wesley's works and found him to be very conscious about living a holy life for Christ. We must never become so engrossed with our personal theologies and lose sight of how to live out the Christian life each day. We want others to see Christ in our life.)*

The first two verses in this chapter are a direct appeal for dedication. *I beseech,* or the Greek *parakaleo*, carries with it the meaning of *strong encouragement.* One of the key words is *therefore* and shows that Paul is drawing a specific conclusion from what he has previously stated. The believers in Rome were to live a *sacrificial life* for Christ in response to the *mercies*, the Greek *oiktirmos*, or the *compassion and favor of God;* that had been shown to them through the free salvation they had received. Only by *God's mercies* each day can anyone live the Christian life. They were a redeemed people, and they could live the way God wanted them to. God never gives us the exhortation to do something without giving us the *mercies* and grace to do it. Once someone has been born again of the Holy Spirit, he has the spiritual power and authority to live a godly life.

Paul's strong use of words is connected to being a ★ slave to Christ, which he had chosen to become. Jesus Christ had set him free from the bondage of sin, and he had devoted his life not to give in to his sinful nature. The fact that Paul calls them *"brethren"* shows that this is a commitment that only believers in Christ can make.

★ *(Paul is drawing from the Old Testament and the Law of Moses. If a slave wanted to continue working for his former master, he would do so as a bondservant. He would receive a mark on his earlobe and remain a bond slave for life.* **Deut. 15:12-18***)*

"that ye present your bodies a living sacrifice, holy, acceptable unto God, which is your reasonable service." **-** Unlike the sacrifices that were offered to God under the old covenant, the believers can now *present their bodies as a living sacrifice.* The sacrifices under the old Levitical system were slain before they were presented to God. The believers in Christ can present their ★ *bodies as a living sacrifice.* Their bodies were no longer the instruments of unrighteousness because they no longer were a part of this evil world. If they voluntarily dedicated their entire lives, this would be *holy and acceptable, or well pleasing* to the Lord. When we consider the cost of what Jesus did for us on the cross, and having been given the promise that one day we will be in heaven with Him, it is our *reasonable service.* This is a mark of true discipleship!

★ *(In the minds of first century Gentiles, they considered the body so unspiritual that they would have never thought of presenting their bodies to God. Paul is showing them here that God is concerned about our bodies. The body of the believer becomes the temple of the living God.* **2 Cor. 6:16***)*

"And be not conformed to this world:" **-** The negative aspect is that a believer in Christ should not ★ *conform* to the world system around him that is controlled by Satan. If the Roman world in the first century was in total contrast to the Christian life, then how much more is the world we live in today, centuries later? The culture around us is in rebellion against Christ and His kingdom.

★ *(Christian living is not a simple, automatic transition from defeat to victory. It is a process of spiritual change that is accomplished by the Holy Spirit. We were sanctified when Jesus saved us; we are being sanctified each day; and one day we will be sanctified forever. This present evil world becomes less and less attractive as we grow in Christ.)*

"but be ye transformed by the renewing of your mind, that ye may prove what is that good, and acceptable, and perfect, will of God." - The positive aspect is that in order for the believer to know the *will of God,* he must *reprogram his mind.* The Greek word here for *"transformed"* is ★ *"metamorphoo,"* which means *"metamorphosis."* This is accomplished by staying in God's Word because the mind of God is revealed in the Sacred Scriptures. As a follower of Jesus, we need to *transform* our thinking to the way that ★★ God thinks.

★ *(The same word is used when Jesus is transfigured in Mark 9:2-3, and also when Paul refers to us being one day changed into the image of the glory of the Lord in* **2 Corinthians 3:18**.*)*

★★ *(One of our prayers should be that God would illuminate our minds with the Eternal Mind of God that is accomplished by the filling of the Holy Spirit.)*

> ***That ye put off concerning the former conversation the old man, which is corrupt according to the deceitful lusts; And be renewed in the spirit of your mind; And that ye put on the new man, which after God is created in righteousness and true holiness.*** **Ephesians 4:22-24**

And have put on the new man, which is renewed in knowledge after the image of him that created him: **Colossians 3:10**

When our minds have been *transformed*, we can *examine* the things around us and *discern* what is the *acceptable and perfect will of God*. There is a *perfect will of God* and a secondary will of God. God has a wonderful plan for each of us, but we must reject the world in order to find it. This is the abundant life that our Lord told us about:

The thief cometh not, but for to steal, and to kill, and to destroy: I am come that they might have life, and that they might have it more abundantly. **John 10:10**

The truths in these first two verses in **Romans 12** are so powerful and so important when it comes to living the Christian life, we need to look at them closely before we move on:

- ***By the mercies of God***
- ***Present your bodies a living sacrifice, holy, acceptable unto God***
- ***Which is your reasonable service***
- ***Be not conformed to this world***
- ***But be ye transformed by the renewing of your mind***
- ***That ye may prove what is that good, and acceptable, and perfect will of God***

Romans 12:3 - ***For I say, through the grace given unto me, to every man that is among you, not to think of himself more highly than he ought to think;***

but to think soberly, according as God hath dealt to every man the measure of faith.

Now Paul makes the appeal for humility that is the result of a believer who has renewed his mind. The appeal goes out to *every believer* and is a word against ★ pride or self-exaltation. Because Paul is about to mention spiritual gifts, there would be a tendency to be lifted up or to think more *highly of one's self than he ought to think.* Just because some had been given more noticeable gifts, and some of the gifts may seem more important, there is no reason for pride. It is God who hath given the gifts and has allotted to each believer a *measure of faith.* Paul is admonishing the believers in Rome to think *soberly,* or the Greek, *sophroneo, to exercise self-control.* Just because someone has been given certain gifts, it does not mean that he is mature in the faith.

★ *(The Apostle Paul had experienced what it was to stay humble before the Lord. Because of the many revelations that God had given to Paul, there was still the tendency for him to be lifted up. God allowed a thorn in the flesh to keep Paul humble.* **2 Corinthians 12:7-9***)*

Romans 12:4-5 - ***For as we have many members in one body, and all members have not the same office: So we, being many, are one body in Christ, and every one members one of another.***

Just as a human body has many parts, so does the assembly of believers. Even though the Church has distinct individuals, the Church is *one whole body in Christ.* While everyone within the Church has different gifts, the ground is level at the cross. Not one believer has ALL of the gifts. We should respect each other. Each believer has a position *in Christ!* We not only belong to Christ, but we belong *to one another.* Each believer has a special gift that is to help edify the body of Christ. We should not try to perform the same function as someone else, but through the mercy of God try to reach our potential with the unique gift that God has given to us.

> **Romans 12:6-8 - *Having then gifts differing according to the grace that is given to us, whether prophecy, let us prophesy according to the proportion of faith; Or ministry, let us wait on our ministering: or he that teacheth, on teaching; Or he that exhorteth, on exhortation: he that giveth, let him do it with simplicity; he that ruleth, with diligence; he that sheweth mercy, with cheerfulness.***

Spiritual gifts are not given because we deserve them, but because of the *grace of God*; therefore, it leaves no room for pride. While there is diversity, there should be harmony. It is interesting here that Paul does *not* list the gift of being an *apostle*, because that was a closed group of 14 individuals who were identified. **(Acts 1:13, 14:14, 21:16)**

While the gift of apostleship was not in the Roman community of believers, the gift of *prophecy* was. Paul warns that someone who is *prophesying* should do so *according to the proportion of faith.* The *prophecy* they give must be ★ tested against the established truths of the faith. In a biblical understanding, to *prophecy* is not necessarily *"fore-telling"* the future but is a *"forth-telling"* of what God has already said. The idea of flippantly saying *"The Lord told me,"* must be tested with what has already been written in God's Word.

★ *(It helps to understand that the Roman communities did not have church buildings or preachers behind a pulpit. The word pulpit comes from the Latin word, "pulpitum" and did not come along until the 9th century AD. The Roman communities met in an open forum, or within a house church setting. The young communities were to test and to make sure that someone was not telling the believers something that went contrary to biblical truth.)*

"Or ministry, let us wait on our ministering:" - The Greek word for *ministry* is *diakonia*, which means *"waiting on tables,"* and where we get the English word for *"deacon."* **(Acts 6:2)** The service within the Church was needed to minister to the widows, orphans, and the sick. They should try not to serve the other members in a hasty way, but wait on the proper time and serve with humility in the name of the Lord.

"or he that teacheth, on teaching" - The gift of *teaching*, or *didasko*, means *to direct or to admonish,* and helps others to understand biblical truth in a clear manner. The word does not mean that there was only one *teacher* in the Roman communities, but the gift of teaching in a general sense.

"Or he that exhorteth, on exhortation:" - The Greek word for *exhorteth* is ★ *parakaleo*, and it means *"to call, summons, or encourage."* This gift would call the people to practice what they had already been taught. A believer cannot just hear God's Word; he is called to ★★ apply the truths to his daily life.

★ *(It is interesting that this word comes from the root word "kaleo" that is used in* **Romans 8:30** *for the word "called.")*

** *(When an individual believer or a congregation only hears God's Word, they never produce spiritual fruit. When a believer has the exhortation to do something that is not biblical truth, he has no depth and will work in the wrong places without acting upon faith.)*

"he that giveth, let him do it with simplicity;" **-** The word for *simplicity* here is haplotes, and means *sincerity or graciousness.* This gift is applicable to all who *give* and is never called a gift anywhere else in Paul's epistles. We should not give with the idea that we have given enough, or measured out a worthy amount, but go beyond and give generously and graciously. Jesus Christ is our prime example:

> ***For ye know the grace of our Lord Jesus Christ, that, though he was rich, yet for your sakes he became poor, that ye through his poverty might be rich.*** **2 Corinthians 8:9**

"he that ruleth, with diligence; he that sheweth mercy, with cheerfulness." **-** The word for *diligence* is *spoude*, and means *"haste or enthusiasm."* If anyone has the gift of *leadership*, he should not be lethargic or unfocused. He needs to vigorously apply himself and be thoughtful of the other believers. There will always be those times when there will be members whose circumstances will be stressful and difficult. Because Christ has given us *mercy*, we should show *mercy* with *graciousness* to those people. Being merciful to others is a characteristic of a kingdom person.

> ***Blessed are the merciful: for they shall obtain mercy.*** **Matthew 5:7**

A Christian's Conduct to Others

Romans 12:9-16 - ***Let love be without dissimulation. Abhor that which is evil; cleave to that which is good. Be kindly affectioned one to another with brotherly love; in honour preferring one another; Not slothful in business; fervent in spirit; serving the Lord; Rejoicing in hope; patient in tribulation; continuing instant in prayer; Distributing to the necessity of saints; given to hospitality. Bless them which persecute you: bless, and curse not. Rejoice with them that do rejoice, and weep with them that weep. Be of the same mind one toward another. Mind not high things, but condescend to men of low estate. Be not wise in your own conceits.***

Here Paul is dealing with the believer's conduct toward those within the believing community in Rome. The first few words, *"Let love unfeigned"* are a heading for what follows. There is no verb in the original, and sincere love *without hypocrisy* connects to the self-explanatory verses that follow. As we study this section, it is very easy to understand why the Church is in spiritual trouble in our world today.

True love *has a horror for* what is evil and is *glued* to *that which is good.* Believers are to show each other a *family love* and be tender toward each other. They are to surpass one another in giving *preference or honor* to the other. We are commanded to do good to all men, but there is a special emphasis to the household of faith. **(Galatians 6:10)** Out of their *deep, passionate service to the Lord* himself, the believers should be *earnest and zealous* and not be *lazy* about their spiritual duties. Their responsibilities in the Church should not be taken lightly. If they will live in *hope or anticipation* of what has been promised them, they will not lose their *joy*. The believer in Christ can *endure persecution, or affliction* if he *continues in prayer. Prayer* is not just a religious ritual, but part of the relationship he has with his Heavenly Father. He is to participate in the ⋆ *needs of the saints.*

⋆ *(According to the first Church in Jerusalem, they even sold their possessions and distributed them to those who had need.* **(Acts 2:42–47)** *Jesus said that we were to make friends with unrighteous mammon or money in* **Luke 16:9.***)*

A follower of Jesus should *seek out* or *pursue* other brethren to show them *hospitality*. Many Christians who traveled benefited greatly from the hospitality of their fellow-Christians since accommodations were poor in those days. As they were to bless God for all that He had done for them, they were to remember the days when they were lost, and *bless those that persecute them.* **(Matthew 5:46)** The people of God are to be a people of blessing and be a witness to the lost world around them. The Apostle Peter said this:

> ***Finally, be ye all of one mind, having compassion one of another, love as brethren, be pitiful, be courteous: Not rendering evil for evil, or railing for railing: but contrariwise blessing; knowing that ye are thereunto called, that ye should inherit a blessing.*** **I Peter 3:8-9**

Those who profess the name of Jesus are to *rejoice with those who rejoice.* If another believer is happy about something, other believers are to join in and be happy with him and not have an envious spirit. If someone within the assembly suffers a loss or a tragedy, he is to *weep with him.* A believer who has true love for the brethren will have deep, inner feelings for others and desire the very best for them, instead of trying to outdo the other believer. Jesus said these words:

> ***Therefore all things whatsoever ye would that men should do to you, do ye even so to them: for this is the law and the prophets.*** **Matthew 7:12** *(Read Leviticus 19:18, 34)*

Believers are not to be *haughty in mind* and only concerned about their own selfish desires. We need to keep a sober mind on what we are and where the Lord has brought us. We cannot accomplish anything without the Lord's grace and mercy. Instead of aiming for a high status in society, they were to associate with *the humble people,* as Jesus did. A Christian should always be reminded of what Jesus said in the story of the *Rich Man and Lazarus.* **(Luke 16:19-31)** There was and still is the danger for Christians to get entangled and become a *"social climber"* and lose sight of what Christ has called them to be. It is very easy to become *wise in our own eyes.*

> ***Be not wise in thine own eyes: fear the Lord, and depart from evil.*** **Proverbs 3:7**

Christian Conduct Toward Unbelievers

> **Romans 12:17-21** - ***Recompense to no man evil for evil. Provide things honest in the sight of all men. If it be possible, as much as lieth in you, live peaceably with all men. Dearly beloved, avenge not yourselves, but rather give place unto wrath: for it is***

> ***written, Vengeance is mine; I will repay, saith the Lord. Therefore if thine enemy hunger, feed him; if he thirst, give him drink: for in so doing thou shalt heap coals of fire on his head. Be not overcome of evil, but overcome evil with good.***

How should the followers of Christ conduct themselves outside the fellowship of the Church? Paul gives six exhortations:

"Recompense to no man evil for evil" **–** It does not take a strong Christian to only show mercy and kindness to fellow brethren, but the test is how we treat our enemies. The Greek word for *"no man"* is *"medeis"* and it means *"no one, nothing."* There is no exception! The impulse of our human nature is to "get even" with those who have wronged us. We must remember that we are to reflect the goodness of Christ to those around us. Take note of what our Lord Jesus said:

> ***Ye have heard that it hath been said, An eye for an eye, and a tooth for a tooth: But I say unto you, That ye resist not evil: but whosoever shall smite thee on thy right cheek, turn to him the other also. And if any man will sue thee at the law, and take away thy coat, let him have thy cloak also. And whosoever shall compel thee to go a mile, go with him twain. Give to him that asketh thee, and from him that would borrow of thee turn not thou away. Ye have heard that it hath been said, Thou shalt love thy neighbour, and hate thine enemy. But I say unto you, Love your enemies, bless them that curse you, do good to them that hate you, and pray for***

them which despitefully use you, and persecute you; That ye may be the children of your Father which is in heaven: for he maketh his sun to rise on the evil and on the good, and sendeth rain on the just and on the unjust. **Matthew 5:38-45**

"Provide things honest in the sight of all men." - The believers in Rome were to give forethought about their actions even to the lost individual. Their personal affairs, family affairs, business affairs, and social affairs are an extension and should be held under scrutiny. Since the people outside of the faith do not understand who Jesus is and are not people of the Holy Bible, we are to make sure that our conduct is *honest and good in the sight of all men.*

"If it be possible, as much as lieth in you, live peaceably with all men." - While the follower of Jesus lives in contrast to the world, we do not seek out contention. A Christian should not be the one who is causing trouble, and he should always strive to *make peace with all men,* even when he feels that he is innocent. He should take the initiative to mend the relationship. Paul realized that it would *not always be possible* in the evil world in which they lived. **(John 16:33)**

"Dearly beloved, avenge not yourselves, but rather give place unto wrath: for it is written, Vengeance is mine; I will repay, saith the Lord." - When a Christian faces injustice and undeserved mistreatment in one form or another, he is not to pursue *revenge.* He must leave room for God's *wrath* to deal with that person. Paul is referring to **Deut. 32:35,** and wants the Roman believers to know what *saith the Lord!* The Lord knows how and when to repay the evil person for his actions.

We are to leave the payback to Him; the God of the Bible is a God of justice! We are not to return *evil for evil,* and we should not execute judgment on anyone.

"Therefore if thine enemy hunger, feed him; if he thirst, give him drink: for in so doing thou shalt heap coals of fire on his head." - Paul is connecting the words in **Deuteronomy** to the truth found in **Proverbs**. Notice that Pauls' words are almost directly quoted from the Old Testament words shown here:

> ***If thine enemy be hungry, give him bread to eat; and if he be thirsty, give him water to drink: For thou shalt heap coals of fire upon his head, and the Lord shall reward thee.*** **Proverbs 25:21-22**

When we do good to our enemies, our motive needs to be pure and prayerfully bring the lost person to repentance, not to condemn him. *Coals of fire upon his head* is an idiom that goes as far back as the Egyptian culture, referring to the *burning conviction* that our kindness places on our enemies. It is interesting that Paul is using this phrase to teach the believers in Rome that *feeding your enemies* will show them the love of Jesus, and the *Lord shall reward thee.* We are to seek opportunities to do good to our enemies. God sees our faith in Christ, but the lost world sees our deeds in our everyday lives.

"Be not overcome of evil, but overcome evil with good." - Even in practical ways we can *overcome evil by doing good.* We should not let the *evil* that is within a person outside of the faith control our attitudes and actions. When we obey the way that Jesus told us to live in **Matthew 5-7**, we can overcome evil and live a triumphant life!

CHAPTER THIRTEEN

THE BELIEVER AND GOVERNMENT

Romans 13:1 - *Let every soul be subject unto the higher powers. For there is no power but of God: the powers that be are ordained of God.*

The fact that the Roman believers were part of the body of Christ did not exempt them from their natural responsibilities, particularly those that were imposed by the government. The Greek word for *"soul"* is *"psuche,"* or *"self, human person, individual."* The believers still lived in a physical world, and Paul wanted to silence anyone who might be within the Roman community who was a ★ radical and thought he could go against the governing authorities or higher powers. Why? God has ★★ *ordained the higher powers;* sometimes to bless the people, and sometimes to judge the people. He not only allows them to rule, but also arranges it. The Greek verb for *"ordained"* is *"tasso,"* meaning *"to determine, to appoint"* and much like the English phrase, *"put in place."*

And he changeth the times and the seasons: he removeth kings, and setteth up kings: he giveth

> ***wisdom unto the wise, and knowledge to them that know understanding:* Daniel 2:21**

★ *(There was a group in Jesus' time called the "Zealots," who was started in 6AD by Judas of Galilee.* **(Acts 5:37)** *They not only refused to pay taxes to the Romans, but they also incited others to fight against Rome. It is interesting that one of Jesus' disciples had been a zealot.* **(Acts 1:13)** *Jesus did not come to fight the Romans. He used them not only to fulfill the Sacred Scriptures, but he also used their infrastructure of roads and seaports to spread the gospel in the first century.)*

★★ *(God used the Romans, Pontius Pilate, Herod, and the corrupt Jewish authorities to crucify Jesus, thus fulfilling the scriptures. The Apostle Paul lived during the time of the wicked Nero, the worst Roman Emperor, and yet he never reviled his authority.)*

> **Romans 13:2 - *Whosoever therefore resisteth the power, resisteth the ordinance of God: and they that resist shall receive to themselves damnation.***

Unless the government ordered the believers to do something in contradiction to God's law, they were bound to obey them. **(Acts 5:29)** God has placed people in positions to rule the nations for His purposes. When a Christian ★ *resisteth the powers, he is resisting the ordinance of God.* The word here for *"damnation"* is *"krima,"* and does not refer to eternal judgment, but a momentary punishment by the law.

★ *(The question may arise, "At what point are we allowed to rebel against high authority?" It is when the government reaches a point where it is promoting evil in order to destroy the good. There were Jews in Nazi Germany during World War II who thought that because this verse was in the Bible, they should not hide the Jews from Adolph Hitler. This is a misapplication of the text.)*

> **Romans 13:3-4 -** ***For rulers are not a terror to good works, but to the evil. Wilt thou then not be afraid of the power? do that which is good, and thou shalt have praise of the same: For he is the minister of God to thee for good. But if thou do that which is evil, be afraid; for he beareth not the sword in vain: for he is the minister of God, a revenger to execute wrath upon him that doeth evil.***

The responsibility of the state and the government is to preserve moral order. Believers in Christ are to live a decent, moral life that does not bring reproach on the name of Jesus. The ruling authorities do not have to be a *terror* for believers because the rulers are actually *ministers of God.* The word *minister* has caused some debate over the centuries. The answer can be resolved when we look at the original word. The Greek word for *"minister"* here is *"diakonos,"* and means *"servant, administrator."* This word can be either a believer in Jesus or an unbeliever. Paul is not referring to the spiritual state of the person, but the position of governmental authority.

"for he beareth not the sword in vain" - In the Roman world criminals were typically executed by beheading with a ★ *sword.* When the state of government punishes evildoers, it is acting as God's servant as an instrument of vengeance *through* whom God is executing His wrath on human sin.

★ *(Then said Jesus unto him, Put up again thy sword into his place: for all they that take the sword shall perish with the sword.)* **Matthew 26:52**

> **Romans 13:5-7 - *Wherefore ye must needs be subject, not only for wrath, but also for conscience sake. For for this cause pay ye tribute also: for they are God's ministers, attending continually upon this very thing. Render therefore to all their dues: tribute to whom tribute is due; custom to whom custom; fear to whom fear; honour to whom honour.***

Another reason why the Christians were commanded by Paul to obey the higher authorities was to keep a *clear conscience.* When we violate our *conscience* regarding good and evil, it gets very difficult to listen to the Holy Spirit. Our *conscience* serves as a spiritual alarm alerting the believer when he has acted against God's Word. While the state or government may be corrupt, a believer in Christ should still ★ *pay tribute, or taxes.* The word for *"ministers"* here is *"leitourgos"* and means *"public servants,"* which is a different word from **verse 4.** Because these **public servants** are devoted to running the government, *taxes* have to be paid.

★ *(Our Lord Jesus performed a miracle of placing a coin in the mouth of a fish that would pay both the tribute for Himself and Simon Peter. This is the only miracle that Jesus performed to keep from offending people.* **Matthew 17:24-27***)*

"tribute to whom tribute is due; custom to whom custom; fear to whom fear; ★ honour to whom honour." - Paul listed four things that define this principle:

★ ***Pay tribute to the government***

★ ***Pay import duties to the custom authorities***

★ ***A middle level fear to the local authorities***

★ ***Show a higher level of honor to the imperial rulers***

★ *(Jesus said to "Render unto Caesar the things that are Caesar's, and unto God the things that are God's."* **(Matthew 22:17-21)** *The spiritual lesson is that Caesar's image was on the coin, but God's image is upon the people. We give our government what is due, but first and foremost we give God ourselves.)*

Christian's Private Obligations

Romans 13:8-10 - *Owe no man any thing, but to love one another: for he that loveth another hath fulfilled the law. For this, Thou shalt not commit adultery, Thou shalt not kill, Thou shalt not steal, Thou shalt not bear false witness, Thou shalt not covet; and if there be any other commandment, it is briefly comprehended in this saying, namely, Thou shalt love thy neighbour as thyself. Love worketh no ill to his neighbour: therefore love is the fulfilling of the law.*

When a believer in Jesus is motivated by love, he will want to fulfill the obligations that are found in the Sacred Scriptures. While there are dangers given in the Bible when we borrow money, **(Prov. 22:7, Matthew 5:42)** this is not the sense of what Paul is saying here. We can never be out of debt when it comes to *loving others.* This is true in the Law of Moses and the Law of Christ:

Thou shalt not avenge, nor bear any grudge against the children of thy people, but thou shalt love thy neighbour as thyself: I am the Lord. **Leviticus 19:18**

And the second is like unto it, Thou shalt love thy neighbour as thyself. **Matthew 22:39**

For all the law is fulfilled in one word, even in this; Thou shalt love thy neighbour as thyself. **Galatians 5:14**

If ye fulfil the royal law according to the scripture, Thou shalt love thy neighbour as thyself, ye do well: **James 2:8**

Paul only quotes the ⋆ *five* commandments that deal with man's relationship to others. It is very important to note that Paul used the Law in the epistle of Romans when describing how Jews and Gentiles are saved *without* the Law. Paul did not want the Gentile believers to think they could live without the moral standards of the Law. When Jesus puts His love in our hearts toward other people, this is how we *fulfill of the Law of love.*

⋆ *(It is interesting that Paul referred to Laws pertaining to our relationship to other people to prove his point about loving one another. Jesus quoted almost the same Laws when confronting the Rich Young Ruler who loved his money more than God or people.* **Matthew 19:16-22**. *Again, we see that the Law is to reveal our faults so we can see our need of Christ.)*

A Sense of Urgency

Romans 13:11-14 - And that, knowing the time, that now it is high time to awake out of ⋆ sleep: for now is

our salvation nearer than when we believed. The night is far spent, the day is at hand: let us therefore cast off the works of darkness, and let us put on the armour of light. Let us walk honestly, as in the ** day; not in rioting and drunkenness, not in chambering and wantonness, not in strife and envying. But put ye on the Lord Jesus Christ, and make not provision for the flesh, to fulfil the lusts thereof.

Our love toward others is to be motivated by the realization that our final destiny is not far away. The Greek word here for *"time"* is *"kairos"* and is found in several other places when referring to eschatological contexts.

* *(Using the image of sleeping when people should be watching was used by Jesus in* **Mark 13:35-36**.*)*

** *(Paul believed that he would see the Return of Christ in his lifetime. He used the contrast of the saved people being children of light to the children of darkness in* **I Thess. 5:4-8**.*)*

"for now is our salvation nearer than when we believed." **-** Once a believer has received the righteousness of Christ, he has started the process of being *delivered* from sin's impact on his life. Our present state is just a taste, or the firstfruits, of the eternal realization. The consummation of this deliverance will be accomplished at the coming of Christ to receive us. His coming is much *nearer* than it was when we were first delivered.

"The night is far spent, the day is at hand: let us therefore cast off the works of darkness, and let us put on the armour of light. Let us walk honestly, as in the day; not in rioting and drunkenness, not in chambering and wantonness, not in strife and envying." **-** The believer is to exchange the *clothes* *of darkness and put on the clothes of light.* We are children of the day and we are to wear the *armour of light* in our daily spiritual battle. Believers should not be living a life of *rioting*, or *komos*, which means *reveling or feasting.* When we consider the time is drawing near, we should not be involved in *chambering*, or *koite*, or *immoral sexual intercourse in bed,* and *wantonness*, or *aselgeia*, which means *outrageous conduct that is even shocking to the public.* This kind of ★ lifestyle leads to *fighting and jealousy.*

★ *(Christianity's teaching concerning sexuality went against the Roman culture and goes against the sexual revolution that the world is seeing today. The believers in Rome, like Christians today, need to understand that morality is a blessing and not a curse. Christians in the first century suffered greatly for their beliefs about marriage and sexuality and were seen as destabilizing to the culture. While some may think that Paul's words are extreme, it helps to understand how open sin was considered the norm in the Roman world.)*

"But put ye on the Lord Jesus Christ, and make not provision for the flesh, to fulfil the lusts thereof." **-** We are to ★ *clothe ourselves* with Jesus Christ! The believer is not to make *provision for the flesh to fulfill the lusts of the flesh.* Believers are not to spend time thinking about how they can gratify the flesh, but cultivate a spiritual perspective about life. While it is impossible to live a life of sinless perfection in the flesh, we should strive to live as close to Jesus as possible. The way we master the desires of the flesh is to place our focus on the person of the Son of God Himself! While Jesus lives inside of the believer through the Holy Spirit, the flesh fights against the Spirit. Paul had experienced that he could not live the Christian life, but that it was Christ living in him:

For to me to live is Christ, and to die is gain. **Philippians 1:21**

I am crucified with Christ: nevertheless I live; yet not I, but Christ liveth in me: and the life which I now live in the flesh I live by the faith of the Son of God, who loved me, and gave himself for me. **Galatians 2:20**

★ *(This author recalls a service in years gone by when an old minister walked up to the platform, took his coat off, and wrapped it around the pulpit. He began to preach on how a Christian puts on the Lord Jesus Christ after he has been born again. It is one thing to be a saved individual and to be on his way to heaven, but it is quite another to live the Christian life while on this earth.)*

CHAPTER FOURTEEN

Attitude Toward the Weaker Christian

> **Romans 14:1-3 -** ***Him that is weak in the faith receive ye, but not to doubtful disputations. For one believeth that he may eat all things: another, who is weak, eateth herbs. Let not him that eateth despise him that eateth not; and let not him which eateth not judge him that eateth: for God hath received him.***

We need to be reminded that Paul was writing this epistle from Corinth, where there were many divisions and carnal Christians. He did not want the Jew and Gentile believers in Rome to have the same problems. When they have someone in their community who is *weak in the faith,* they are to accept him/her with tenderness and love. They are to receive him/her not for the purpose of judging or correcting, but as brother and sister in Christ. The *weak in faith* are not necessarily weaker in their love for the Lord, but *stricter* in the way they live their daily lives. Several things may cause a Christian to be *weak in the faith:*

★ ***They may be babes in Christ*** *(young believers)*

★ ***They may be carnal*** *(worldly)*

★ ***They may have fallen into ★ legalism*** *(Touch not, taste not, handle not,* **Col. 2:21***)*

★ ***They may not have been under sound teachings***

★ ***They held to the Jewish dietary laws***

★ *(Legalism is living by a set of rules that are not found in the Sacred Scriptures and then enforcing these rules on other believers. The danger is that legalism mimics spirituality and makes people look religious on the outside. This was the case with Judaism in Paul's day and also the Christian Church in modern day. Sometimes people are accepted within a certain church, and then they turn around and condemn the ones who have accepted them. Man-made rules that are not founded in the Bible are optional and not mandatory. Legalism has a way of making us think that we are stronger than other believers.)*

Paul provides an application with *eating or not eating certain things.* Some believers have no convictions about eating everything. They do not stumble over certain foods, and feel a total freedom to partake of what they desire. There are others who restrict themselves to *herbs*, or the Greek *lachanon*, meaning *garden vegetables,* and do not partake of eating meat. Possibly they thought that the meat had been offered to pagan gods. **(I Cor. 8)** Paul is primarily concerned with the believer's *attitude* toward those that he calls *weak in the faith.* They are not to judge weak believers as being narrow-minded. On the other hand, those who choose not to eat certain foods are ★ not to judge those who eat everything. The reason is that God has *received* both the strong believer and the weak believer in Christ, and everyone is at a different level in his walk and has a different preference to foods.

★ *(This author was working in Israel years ago on a television project with a producer who was a Jewish Christian. He would condemn us for eating certain foods and not keeping certain holy days, and yet he thought it was fine for him to drink alcohol every night during meals. While we did not think that it was a sin for him to consume alcoholic beverages, he was not consistent or thoughtful about our convictions.)*

> **Romans 14:4 -** ***Who art thou that judgest another man's servant? to his own master he standeth or falleth. Yea, he shall be holden up: for God is able to make him stand.***

Only a master has the right to pronounce *judgment on his own servant.* A believer should not pass judgment upon another believer who, in fact, is *God's house servant.* Some stricter-minded Christians may think a believer should or should not be doing something because it would lead them into sin and *they would fall.* God is certainly strong enough *to hold the believer up and make him to stand.* Paul is telling the believers in Rome to rise above silly and bigoted things. Unless it is a scriptural issue or an immoral issue, we are not to ★ judge other believers. It is God's place to judge His servants, not ours!

★ *(There is certainly a time and place for Christians to judge.* **Matthew 18:18, I Cor. 5:1-5***)*

> **Romans 14:5-6 -** ***One man esteemeth one day above another: another esteemeth every day alike. Let every man be fully persuaded in his own mind. He that regardeth the day, regardeth it unto the Lord;***

and he that regardeth not the day, to the Lord he doth not regard it. He that eateth, eateth to the Lord, for he giveth God thanks; and he that eateth not, to the Lord he eateth not, and giveth God thanks.

What Paul said concerning eating different foods could also be said concerning certain days that the Jews may have *esteemed* religious, while the Gentile believers in Rome may have used their Christian liberty not to observe these days. The key phrases are *persuaded in his own mind* and *to the Lord.* A person who observes a specific day or who does not eat certain foods is doing this *in reference to the Lord.* If a person feels the liberty to eat all foods and does not observe certain days also is doing this in reference to the Lord. Both are giving *thanks to the Lord* for all things. Paul is trying to press home the thought that believers are free in the Messiah, and each individual should examine his own heart to ensure that he is doing what he believes the Lord would have him to do. Yet, he does not have the right to judge other believers on the basis of what they *eat* or what *day* they observe.

Most likely there were differences of opinions about what *day* of the week they were to gather together to worship. Possibly some of the Jewish believers had convictions about worshipping on the ⋆ *Sabbath Day,* while some of the Gentile believers felt the *First Day of the Week,* or also called *"The Lord's Day"* would be the appropriate day. **(Acts 20:7, I Cor. 16:2, Rev. 1:10)**

⋆ *(The Sabbath Day has caused much confusion within the body of Christ over the centuries. The answer can be found when we carefully study the Old Testament. The Sabbath Day was not observed between Adam and Moses, and is not mentioned in the book of Job.*

The Sabbath Day was for a sign between God and Israel and was observed between Moses and Jesus. **Nehemiah 9:14** *mentions that the Sabbath began with Moses.* **(Ezekiel 20:12, 20)** *There was a prophecy that the Sabbath Day would cease in* **Hosea 2:11.** *The Sabbath Day was a shadow of things to come.* **Colossians 2:16-17***)*

> **Romans 14:7-9 - *For none of us liveth to himself, and no man dieth to himself. For whether we live, we live unto the Lord; and whether we die, we die unto the Lord: whether we live therefore, or die, we are the Lord's. For to this end Christ both died, and rose, and revived, that he might be Lord both of the dead and living.***

We are reminded here that from the beginning of our earthly life until the end, we are connected to other believers. We are not like an island! Believers belong to the Lord both in life and in death. Our first responsibility is to the Lord, and we need to be sensitive to what pleases Him. Jesus Christ is Lord over life and death because He became the *God-Man.* Jesus the Son of God was born; lived a sinless life on earth; willingly died on a cross; was buried; and ★ rose again to live forevermore, proving that He is the Lord! The Greek phrasing here is unusual and difficult to translate: *"Christ both died as well as rose and lived."* Therefore, He is qualified to exercise Lordship and judgment. Each Christian needs to be careful how he judges others. Even though we may disagree about eating habits and observing days, all true believers belong to God!

★ *(The Apostle Paul encountered many who did not believe in a resurrection, specifically at Mars Hill and in the church at Corinth.* **Acts 17:32, I Cor. 15:12***)*

> **Romans 14:10-12 -** ***But why dost thou judge thy brother? or why dost thou set at nought thy brother? for we shall all stand before the judgment seat of Christ. For it is written, As I live, saith the Lord, every knee shall bow to me, and every tongue shall confess to God. So then every one of us shall give account of himself to God.***

While believers do not have the right to judge another believer, the Lord Himself does have the right to judge every believer, whether he is strong or weak in the faith. Every individual who has been redeemed by the blood of Christ will give an account of what he has done in the body, either good or bad. It is not to determine his eternal destiny, but to determine his rewards. This should be a wake-up call for all Christians not to judge others. We will have enough to answer for without judging someone else. The sins of the flesh and the sins of the spirit would be enough to condemn everyone if it were not for the sacrifice of Jesus on the cross. No Christian will be exempt from standing before ★ *the Judgment Seat of Christ.*

> ***For we must all appear before the judgment seat of Christ; that every one may receive the things done in his body, according to that he hath done, whether it be good or bad.*** **2 Cor. 5:10**

> ***Every man's work shall be made manifest: for the day shall declare it, because it shall be revealed by fire; and the fire shall try every man's work of what sort it is. If any man's work abide which he hath built thereupon, he shall receive a reward. If any man's work shall be burned, he shall suffer loss: but he himself shall be saved; yet so as by fire.*** **I Corinthians 3:13-15**

★ *(The participants in the judgment seat of Christ are members of the New Testament Church. These are people who have trusted Christ as Savior from the Day of Pentecost, until the coming of Christ for His Church. This will also determine the believer's position in the Messianic Kingdom. The unbelievers will be judged at the Great White Throne.* **Revelation 20:11-15***)*

"For it is written, As I live, saith the Lord, every knee shall bow to me, and every tongue shall confess to God." **-** This is a powerful connection that Paul is making about the Deity of Christ. Many times we fail to see that the *Jesus* in the New Testament is the same *Lord God* of the Old Testament:

> ***I have sworn by myself, the word is gone out of my mouth in righteousness, and shall not return, That unto me every knee shall bow, every tongue shall swear. Isaiah 45:23***

> ***Wherefore God also hath highly exalted him, and given him a name which is above every name: That at the name of Jesus every knee should bow, of things in heaven, and things in earth, and things under the earth; And that every tongue should***

confess that Jesus Christ is Lord, to the glory of God the Father. **Philippians 2:9-11**

Romans 14:13 - ***Let us not therefore judge one another any more: but judge this rather, that no man put a stumblingblock or an occasion to fall in his brother's way.***

Rather than passing judgment upon other believers, we should be seriously concerned how our deeds will show up when we stand before the *Judgment Seat of Christ.* We need to be passing judgment upon our own behavior. The other side of the coin is that our judgmental actions may cause another believer to *stumble.* Sometimes we forget that some things that we do may not necessarily be sinful, but they can cause another Christian to trip or fall along his journey. There are two ways that we can put a *stumbling block*, or the Greek proskomma, in the way of a fellow believer:

* ***By discouraging them and beating them down through legalism***
* ***By enticing them to sin through an unwise use of our liberty***

Romans 14:14-16 - ***I know, and am persuaded by the Lord Jesus, that there is nothing unclean of itself: but to him that esteemeth any thing to be unclean, to him it is unclean. But if thy brother be grieved with thy meat, now walkest thou not charitably. Destroy not him with thy meat, for whom Christ died. Let not then your good be evil spoken of:***

Under the Mosaic Law were certain foods considered to be *unclean.* They are not *unclean* to the Gentile believers now, and under the present Law of Christ they are *clean.* If a weak believer considers pork, shrimp, lobster, etc., to be *unclean,* it is *unclean* to them. Defilement is not in the food itself, but in the conscience. A Gentile believer may have to limit his freedom in order to exercise the Law of love toward a Jewish believer; *for whom Christ died.* While this is not an *absolute* law here, Paul is saying that in ★ certain situations, the Law of love should be practiced.

★ *(A good illustration would be the use of fermented wine during Communion. Because alcohol is a problem in our society, many churches should ban drinking altogether. It is not a sin to drink wine, but if it causes a stumbling block, then the church should not use wine for the Lord's Supper.)*

"Let not then your good be evil spoken of:" - The Greek word for *"good"* here is *"agathon,"* and it means *"intrinsically good whether others see it good or not."* It has a wider meaning to show that what a stronger believer might enjoy, the weaker believer avoids. If Jesus were willing to give up His life for the sake of our brothers and sisters, then we should be willing to give up a seafood dinner if it offends my brother or sister. If we push our liberty and go ahead and have the seafood dinner, then this could cause the weaker brother to *speak evil* about what we have done.

> **Romans 14:17 -** ***For the kingdom of God is not meat and drink; but righteousness, and peace, and joy in the Holy Ghost.***

It is easy for a Christian to get his priorities in the wrong place. If we start placing *food and drink before righteousness and peace and joy in the Holy Ghost,* then we are out of touch with the Lord. Our minds should be focused on the ★ *kingdom of God!* God's kingdom is made up of all believers who have received Jesus as their personal Savior, and we need to promote harmony among the brethren. It is all about pleasing Jesus, who is the King of the kingdom!

★ *(The Lord Jesus did say that He would partake of wine once again when He returns to establish His physical kingdom in Luke 22:18. There will be eating and drinking in the future kingdom. Paul is speaking about our present experience in the kingdom of God. An example would be when three of the disciples got to experience a glimpse of the glory of God when they saw Jesus transfigured. They were not actually in the literal kingdom.* **Luke 9:27-31, 2 Peter 1:16-19***)*

> **Romans 14:18 -** ***For he that in these things serveth Christ is acceptable to God, and approved of men.***

The continual service of Christ out of a pure heart *honors God* and is *approved*, or the Greek, *dokimos*, or *tested and tried of men.* There is eternal significance to the matter of how we treat our fellow brothers and sisters in Christ. The Lord leaves us on this earth after we are saved in order to promote His kingdom. He wants us to edify the brethren! We need to be reminded that Jesus lives within His people!

> **Romans 14:19-21 -** ***Let us therefore follow after the things which make for peace, and things wherewith one may edify another. For meat destroy not the work of God. All things indeed are pure; but it is evil for***

> ***that man who eateth with offence. It is good neither to eat flesh, nor to drink wine, nor any thing whereby thy brother stumbleth, or is offended, or is made weak.***

While all of this may seem to be an overstatement for we Gentiles today, we must consider again that Jewish Christians were meeting with Gentile Christians almost 2,000 years ago in a totally different culture. Their fellowship with one another was much closer than most of the Gentile Christians are today. Before Paul leaves this subject, he repeats again that the food itself is not impure, but there is nothing *pure* about causing a brother to *stumble.* When our lives are being motivated with the love of God, *we follow after peace and the things that will edify one another.* It was a warning for the Jewish believers, as well as the Gentile believers. If a mature believer in Christ persuades a weaker believer to do that which goes contrary to his own conscience, that makes a good thing evil.

So how well do we know the people we worship beside? How well do we understand them? Do we have convictions about certain things that we have never shared with our closest Christian friends? If we tear down our spiritual brothers and sisters for petty preferences in food or drink, then we are revealing how carnal we really are. Again, Paul is referring to our actions in front of other believers, not in our private lives.

> **Romans 14:22-23 -** ***Hast thou faith? have it to thyself before God. Happy is he that condemneth not himself in that thing which he alloweth. And he that doubteth is damned if he eat, because he eateth not of faith: for whatsoever is not of faith is sin.***

A weak or immature believer who has *faith* does not have to give up his own convictions in his private life. Believers who have a clear conscience on non-moral matters are *happy*, or the Greek, *makarios*, or *blessed, before God.* If God is challenging us to give something up and we still try to approve ourselves, we *condemn ourselves.* Or if God is trying to show us that we need to grow in our *faith* and quit focusing on what others are *eating*, we need to listen to the Lord. We need to be sensitive of the Holy Spirit and be willing to change. Real happiness is found when we walk close to Jesus and not by approving something just because it makes us *happy*, or we were raised to believe it. One way to judge those grey areas in our life – if we cannot do it in *faith, then it is sin.* If something troubles our spirit and we do not have peace about it, we better not do it. It goes back to violating our own conscience. If our actions contradict what we believe the Sacred Scriptures teach, then they are sinful actions. The way we live out the Christian life is by living out what God has impressed upon us from His Word. **(Romans 12:2)**

CHAPTER FIFTEEN

ATTITUDE OF THE STRONG BELIEVERS

> **Romans 15:1-3 - *We then that are strong ought to bear the infirmities of the weak, and not to please ourselves. Let every one of us please his neighbour for his good to edification. For even Christ pleased not himself; but, as it is written, The reproaches of them that reproached thee fell on me.***

Notice here that Paul includes himself with the pronouns we and us. The Greek word for *"strong"* is *"dunatos,"* and it means *"able, mighty, powerful."* The *strong* believers are the ones who are capable of doing something that the weaker believers are not able to do. The word for *"please"* is *"aresko,"* and carries with it *"the willingness to serve others."* Paul is saying that the *strong* believers in Christ should help carry the *weaknesses* of the other believers and take the doubts and hesitations of their brethren upon themselves. The stronger believer is to look out for his *neighbors* or fellow believers not just to *please* them, but to build them up and to edify them. This passage comes to mind:

> ***Let nothing be done through strife or vainglory; but in lowliness of mind let each esteem other better than themselves. Look not every man on his own things, but every man also on the things of others.* Philippians 2:3-4**

As always, Christ is our perfect example, and Paul quotes from the Psalms:

> ***For the zeal of thine house hath eaten me up; and the reproaches of them that reproached thee are fallen upon me.* Psalm 69:9**

This verse relates two different events in the life of Christ. The same Jesus who overturned the moneychangers in the Temple as an expression of His *zeal* **(John 2:17)** willingly went to the cross. The *reproaches*, or the Hebrew, *cherpah*, means the *taunting, shame, scorn,* and *disgrace* that were cast against us and God was laid upon Jesus. Our goal is not to *please our neighbors,* but to bring glory to God by the way we treat them. There is a time to have *zeal* about what is wrong and dishonoring to God, and there is a time to lift up the weaker brother. Jesus is the *Lion of the Tribe of Judah* in **Rev. 5:5,** but He is also the *Suffering Servant* of **Isaiah 53.** Satan's strategy is to use us to tear down the body of Christ. We are supposed to be building up God's kingdom. Placing others first as *Jesus did* is a classic idea that Paul uses in Philippians:

> ***Let this mind be in you, which was also in Christ Jesus: Who, being in the form of God, thought it not robbery to be equal with God: But made himself***

> ***of no reputation, and took upon him the form of a servant, and was made in the likeness of men: And being found in fashion as a man, he humbled himself, and became obedient unto death, even the death of the cross.*** **Philippians 2:5-8**

> **Romans 15:4 -** ***For whatsoever things were written aforetime were written for our learning, that we through patience and comfort of the scriptures might have hope.***

Another principle of glorifying God through unity is based upon the *hope* that we have in the Sacred Scriptures that were *written aforetime for our learning.* The Holy Bible serves many spiritual purposes in our lives, but one main purpose is that it gives us *hope*! The strong or weak believers may not agree on every little issue, but they both can have this *hope.*

Paul is not just referring to specific scriptures, but to *all* of the Old Testament and the ⋆ New Testament writings which already had been written and yet to be written.

> ***Now all these things happened unto them for examples: and they are written for our admonition, upon whom the ends of the world are come.*** **I Corinthians 10:11**

⋆ *(There were several of Paul's letters written before the epistle to the Romans. Matthew and Mark's gospel accounts had already been written along with the book of James.)*

The *hope* that all believers have is the expectation of the ⋆ Second Coming of Jesus Christ. If all of the prophecies written concerning His first coming were fulfilled, then certainly the scriptures pertaining to His Second Coming will be fulfilled. When we consider passages such as **Hebrews 11:** with people like Abel, Enoch, Noah, Abraham, Moses, Rahab, Gideon, Samson, David, and Samuel, we find *encouragement* and the motivation to *endure.* The Old Testament saints looked for a reward even before the Messiah came. How much more *hope* of eternal life should we have after the resurrection of Jesus?

★ *(There are over 1,800 references to the Second Coming of Jesus in the Sacred Scriptures. We know that He fulfilled over 300 direct prophecies during His first coming. There is one in every 30 verses in the New Testament that relates to His return.)*

> **Romans 15:5-6 -** ***Now the God of patience and consolation grant you to be likeminded one toward another according to Christ Jesus: That ye may with one mind and one mouth glorify God, even the Father of our Lord Jesus Christ.***

Paul is giving a prayer for the oneness of the believers in Rome. The two graces of *patience and consolation* are revealed through the Sacred Scriptures. If the Holy Spirit rules in the heart of the believer, then a variety of opinions need not destroy the harmony and unity he can enjoy. The basis for this unity is the fact that it is *according to Christ Jesus.* One of the purposes of salvation is that the body of believers, Jew and Gentile, strong and weak, will have one *mind and* ★ *one mouth in glorifying the Father of our Lord Jesus Christ.*

★ *(This author recalls a morning in Jerusalem when our pilgrimage took us to the Garden Tomb just north of the city to commemorate the resurrection of Christ. On this beautiful morning we entered into the Garden, and the voice of several languages from many parts of the world were praising the Lord. Some of the old church hymns could be heard in different tongues, but they were all in one accord. It was a very moving experience and was a good illustration of how we should not let diversity divide the believers in Christ.)*

Romans 15:7 - *Wherefore receive ye one another, as Christ also received us to the glory of God.*

Since Jesus had received the Jew and Gentile believers in Rome into His kingdom, they should also receive one another. The phrase *Christ also received us,* or the Greek, *proslambano,* is not found any other time in the New Testament. Even though the concept is found in many places, this actual wording is only found here. Jesus has *welcomed us; He has taken us to Himself.* Jesus did not receive us because we were perfect, because He could not see any fault in us, or because He was hoping to gain something in return. He died for us on the cross because we could not save ourselves, and He was thinking about us. Jesus did for us what we could never do for ourselves. Even today, Jesus does not approve of all the things we do and say, but He has *accepted* us! Believers are to ★ *receive one another* in this same way.

★ *(We may not agree on many things that believers may adopt, such as: jewelry, tattoos, the dress code, facial hair, style of music, structure of worship services, dietary laws, and/or observing holy days, but if we believe in Jesus as the Son of God, we should receive one another. We must find unity in the essential truths of the Holy Bible.)*

Jews and Gentiles Glorify God

> **Romans 15:8-9 - *Now I say that Jesus Christ was a minister of the circumcision for the truth of God, to confirm the promises made unto the fathers: And that the Gentiles might glorify God for his mercy; as it is written, For this cause I will confess to thee among the Gentiles, and sing unto thy name.***

Israel's Messiah Jesus was first sent to the *circumcision,* or *the lost sheep of the house of Israel.* **(Matt. 15:24, 10:5-6)** The basis for His ministry was for *the truth of God and to confirm the promises given unto the fathers.* The sign and seal of the Abrahamic Covenant was *circumcision.* Many times Jesus pointed out that what He said and did was a fulfillment of the Old Testament promises. **(Matt. 12:40, 15:1-20, 21:42, 22:44, 26:31, John 5:39-47, 6:31-51, 58, 19:28)** God raised up the Jewish people and the nation of Israel through which the Messiah would come. The Person and Work of Christ fulfilled the Law that was given to Moses:

> ***But when the fulness of the time was come, God sent forth his Son, made of a woman, made under the law, To redeem them that were under the law, that we might receive the adoption of sons.* Galatians 4:4-5**

Israel's Messiah had to be a Jew from the Tribe of Judah, **(Gen. 49:10)** and He came to His brethren in the flesh first. Jesus was the *son of David* (kingly, royal lineage) *and the son of Abraham* (Seed of Abraham that would bless the nations):

> ***The book of the generation of Jesus Christ, the son of David, the son of Abraham.*** **Matthew 1:1**

"And that the Gentiles might glorify God for his mercy; as it is written, For this cause I will confess to thee among the Gentiles, and sing unto thy name." - The Abrahamic Covenant includes physical blessings that were limited to the Jews, but the spiritual blessings were to extend to the *Gentiles so they could glorify God for his mercy.* This blessing was only to the *Gentiles* who embraced Jesus as their Savior. Through the birth of the New Testament Church in **Acts 2**, Jewish and Gentile believers were brought into the body of Christ. The purpose was for the union of glorifying God!

> ***Which in other ages was not made known unto the sons of men, as it is now revealed unto his holy apostles and prophets by the Spirit; That the Gentiles should be fellowheirs, and of the same body, and partakers of his promise in Christ by the gospel:*** **Ephesians 3:5-6**

The Eternal God has designed a plan that would fulfill His promises to the Jews, and through their unbelief would give an opportunity for the Gentiles to give glory to God as well. It was a part of *God's mercy* to mankind! What a glorious mystery!

The Hebrew style of teaching called a *string of pearls* that Paul uses referring to the *Gentiles*, or *heathen*, comes from two passages in the Old Testament. This also proves the significance of every small phrase in the Old Testament:

Therefore I will give thanks unto thee, O Lord, among the heathen, and I will sing praises unto thy name. **2 Samuel 22:50**

Therefore will I give thanks unto thee, O Lord, among the heathen, and sing praises unto thy name. **Psalm 18:49**

Romans 15:10-12 - *And again he saith, Rejoice, ye Gentiles, with his people. And again, Praise the Lord, all ye Gentiles; and laud him, all ye people. And again, Esaias saith, There shall be a root of Jesse, and he that shall rise to reign over the Gentiles; in him shall the Gentiles trust.*

Paul gives a series of quotations from the Hebrew Scriptures to show that it was written centuries earlier that God would show mercy to the Gentiles, and they would praise His name along with the Jews who received their Messiah:

Rejoice, O ye nations, with his people: **Deuteronomy 32:43**

O praise the Lord, all ye nations: praise him, all ye people. **Psalm 117:1**

And in that day there shall be a root of Jesse, which shall stand for an ensign of the people; to it shall the Gentiles seek: and his rest shall be glorious. **Isaiah 11:10**

Contextually, if God has brought union between the Jews and Gentiles through Christ, how much more should the strong and weak believers be able to have a union that will glorify God?

Romans 15:13 - ***Now the God of hope fill you with all joy and peace in believing, that ye may abound in hope, through the power of the Holy Ghost.***

- ***The source of blessing is the God of hope***
- ***The content of the blessing is joy and peace***
- ***The means of receiving this blessing is in believing***
- ***The purpose of the blessing is that they may abound in hope in the power of the Holy Ghost***

Paul's Role in the Gentile World

Romans 15:14-16 - ***And I myself also am persuaded of you, my brethren, that ye also are full of goodness, filled with all knowledge, able also to admonish one another. Nevertheless, brethren, I have written the more boldly unto you in some sort, as putting you in mind, because of the grace that is given to me of God, That I should be the minister of Jesus Christ to the Gentiles, ministering the gospel of God, that the offering up of the Gentiles might be acceptable, being sanctified by the Holy Ghost.***

The reason why Paul has been so *bold* in this epistle is because God had called him to be *the minister of Jesus Christ to the Gentiles.* The word for minister in this verse is *leitourgos,* and it is only found here in the New Testament. The word gives the idea of a *servant, or the official character as the priests and Levites.* While Paul was not within the inner circle of the Apostles who walked with the Son of God, he was given the gift of apostleship. Since the church at Rome had more Gentile believers than Jewish believers, Paul was exercising his apostolic authority to the Gentiles.

As mentioned at the beginning, Paul did not establish the church in Rome, nor had he visited them. He did not think that the believers in Rome were unaware of the things he was teaching them, for he was *persuaded that they were filled with all knowledge able to admonish one another.* The believing community in Rome was not as carnal as the church in *Corinth*, or as easy to be led astray as the churches in *Galatia*. By using the priestly imagery, Paul wanted the Gentile believers in Rome to live in such a godly manner that *their lives would be an offering acceptable by God and sanctified by the Holy Ghost.* As the Apostle Peter would later write, Paul wanted the Jew and Gentile believers in Rome to have an abundant entrance into God's kingdom.

> ***And beside this, giving all diligence, add to your faith virtue; and to virtue knowledge; And to knowledge temperance; and to temperance patience; and to patience godliness; And to godliness brotherly kindness; and to brotherly kindness charity. For if these things be in you, and abound, they make you that ye shall neither be barren nor unfruitful in the knowledge of our Lord Jesus Christ. But he that lacketh these things is blind, and cannot see afar off, and hath forgotten that he was purged from his old sins. Wherefore the rather, brethren, give diligence to make your calling and election sure: for if ye do***

> ***these things, ye shall never fall: For so an entrance shall be ministered unto you abundantly into the everlasting kingdom of our Lord and Saviour Jesus Christ.*** **2 Peter 1:5-11**

> **Romans 15:17-19 -** ***I have therefore whereof I may glory through Jesus Christ in those things which pertain to God. For I will not dare to speak of any of those things which Christ hath not wrought by me, to make the Gentiles obedient, by word and deed, Through mighty signs and wonders, by the power of the Spirit of God; so that from Jerusalem, and round about unto Illyricum, I have fully preached the gospel of Christ.***

Although Paul established churches all over the Roman Empire, perhaps he had grounds for boasting. He wanted them to know that his *glorying was in Jesus Christ in those things pertaining to God.* Paul knew that his success had nothing to do with his natural abilities. His faith, motivation, and zeal came from the calling that God had placed on his life. His duty and success were his priestly offerings to God. He would *never think of speaking anything other than what Jesus had accomplished through him.* Paul's goal was to make the Gentiles obedient to the faith. He did this by preaching the *word to them and by his ⋆ deeds.*

⋆ *(Someone who is called into the ministry of Jesus Christ will not only preach the Word, but his life will be filled with good deeds. "The former treatise have I made, O Theophilus, of all that Jesus began both to do and teach." Acts 1:1)*

"Through mighty signs and wonders, by the power of the Spirit of God; so that from Jerusalem, and round about unto ⋆

Illyricum, I have fully preached the gospel of Christ." - *Signs and wonders* were accomplished by Jesus the Son of God and His Apostles, but they only lasted for a time. Here are some of the *sign miracles* of Paul *by the power of the Spirit of God:*

- ⋆ ***Acts 14:8-10*** - *(Paul healed a man lame from birth in Lystra.)*
- ⋆ ***Acts 16:16-18*** - *(Paul cast a spirit of divination out of a slave girl in Philippi.)*
- ⋆ ***Acts 19:11-12*** - *(Paul healed many who were demon-possessed in Corinth.)*
- ⋆ ***Acts 20:9-12*** - *(Paul raised Eutychus back to life in Troas.)*
- ⋆ ***Acts 28:3-9*** - *(Paul was not harmed after being bitten by a viper, and he healed many people in Malta.)*

⋆ *(The Roman province of Illyricum (present-day Albania) was located on the eastern side of the Adriatic Sea, across from Italy. This province also included the region of Dalmatia mentioned in* **2 Timothy 4:10.** *It has been estimated that the Apostle Paul walked some 10,000 miles from Israel up to Asia Minor, Greece, and Italy, not including his journeys by ship across the Mediterranean, the Aegean, the Adriatic, and Tyrrhenian Seas.)*

Paul had fully, or the Greek *pleroo,* or *"to make full, or complete"* preached the gospel of Christ. Paul not only preached the full gospel, which is the death, burial, and resurrection of Jesus, but he also would *complete* what God had called him to do in his earthly life. He would accomplish the purpose that God had for his life.

> **Romans 15:20-21** - ***Yea, so have I strived to preach the gospel, not where Christ was named, lest I should***

> ***build upon another man's foundation: But as it is written, To whom he was not spoken of, they shall see: and they that have not heard shall understand.***

Paul's *desire* was to *preach*, or *evangelize*, the gospel in places and to people where the *name of Christ* had not been preached. Why? Paul did not want *to build upon another man's* ★*foundation.* He wanted to do a pioneer work for Christ because the world in Paul's time was filled with so many who had never heard the gospel.

★ *(Believers in Christ today are to build on the foundation that was laid by the Apostles.* **Ephesians 2:19-3:6***)*

Paul cites from a verse in *Isaiah* written over seven centuries before. The Hebrew Scriptures of the Old Testament are so profound and so inspired that they would prophecy about the humiliation and *victory* of the coming Messiah in Isaiah's time writing from Jerusalem, while looking ahead to the spreading of the gospel in Paul's time.

> ***So shall he sprinkle many nations; the kings shall shut their mouths at him: for that which had not been told them shall they see; and that which they had not heard shall they consider.*** **Isaiah 52:15**

Paul's Future Plans

> **Romans 15:22-24** - ***For which cause also I have been much hindered from coming to you. But now having no more place in these parts, and having a great desire these many years to come unto you; Whensoever I take my journey into Spain, I will***

> ***come to you: for I trust to see you in my journey, and to be brought on my way thitherward by you, if first I be somewhat filled with your company.***

Paul had been hindered from visiting the church in Rome because of the abundant work in Asia Minor and Greece, and his return to Jerusalem. Because *he had no more places to go* in Greece, Paul had a *yearning affection* to go to Rome. Paul's ultimate plan was to go to ⋆ *Spain*, which was on the outer western limits of the Roman Empire. Having established churches in the eastern part of the empire, he now wished to expand his ministry into the western part. Paul was hoping to be spiritually *filled up* with fellowship with the Roman believers. He needed financial support to travel to *Spain*.

⋆ *(While Paul's immediate plans to go to Spain were interrupted, it is believed that after his release from the first Roman imprisonment at the end of the book of Acts, he did make it to Spain. Clement of Rome, (35-99 AD) who was a co-laborer with Paul,* **(Philippians 4:3)** *became the bishop of Rome. Clement wrote these words about 20 years later:*

> *"Because of jealousy and strife, Paul, by his example, pointed out the way to the prize for patient endurance. After he had been seven times in chains, had been driven into exile, had been stoned and had preached in the East and in the West, he won the genuine glory for his faith, having taught righteousness to the whole world and having reached the farthest limits of the West. Finally, when he had given his testimony before the rulers, he thus departed from the world and went to the holy place, having become an outstanding example of patient endurance."*

Also, Cyril of Jerusalem (313-386 AD), Chrysostom (347-407 AD), and Jerome (342-420 AD) also wrote that Paul did go to Spain.)

> **Romans 15:25-29 - *But now I go unto Jerusalem to minister unto the saints. For it hath pleased them of Macedonia and Achaia to make a certain contribution for the poor saints which are at Jerusalem. It hath pleased them verily; and their debtors they are. For if the Gentiles have been made partakers of their spiritual things, their duty is also to minister unto them in carnal things. When therefore I have performed this, and have sealed to them this fruit, I will come by you into Spain. And I am sure that, when I come unto you, I shall come in the fulness of the blessing of the gospel of Christ.***

Before Paul could begin his journey to Rome, he had to first go to *Jerusalem*, which was over 1,800 miles southeast from Corinth. His first duty was to help the poor saints in Jerusalem by taking an offering that had been collected among the Gentile believers in *Macedonia and* ★ *Achaia.*

★ *(These were Roman provinces in the country of Greece. Corinth, where Paul was located while writing, was within the province of Achaia.)*

There was a theological reason why the Gentiles were giving to the poor Jewish saints in Jerusalem. The Gentiles, who had heard the gospel of Christ, were indebted to the Jewish believers. If the Gentile believers had received so many spiritual blessings from the Jewish Christians in Jerusalem, it was only right for them to help their Jewish brethren in Jerusalem. God had used the Apostle Paul to break down the ethnic barriers and to have compassion on the *saints* in the Body of Christ. The Greek word for *"sealing the fruit"* is "sphragizo," only used here in the New Testament, and carried the idea of *"security or to set a seal upon."* Notice these thoughts:

- ★ ***The tomb of Jesus was sealed – (Matthew 27:66)***
- ★ ***Believers are sealed by the Holy Spirit – (Ephesians 4:30)***
- ★ ***Paul will seal the fruit, or make sure the offering gets to Jerusalem***
- ★ ***The future rewards of the saints in Macedonia and Achaia were sealed***

"And I am sure that, when I come unto you, I shall come in the fulness of the blessing of the gospel of Christ" - Paul would bear the material blessings to the Jewish believers in Jerusalem, and when he comes to Rome, he will *come in the fullness of the blessing of the gospel of Christ.* The good news about the finished work of the Lord Jesus Christ and the hope of His Second Coming would bring a *fullness of blessing!*

Paul's Desire for Prayer

> **Romans 15:30-33** - ***Now I beseech you, brethren, for the Lord Jesus Christ's sake, and for the love of the Spirit, that ye strive together with me in your prayers to God for me; That I may be delivered from them that do not believe in Judaea; and that my service which I have for Jerusalem may be accepted of the saints; That I may come unto you with joy by the will of God, and may with you be refreshed. Now the God of peace be with you all. Amen.***

As great of a Christian as Paul was, he still felt the urgent need to ask the believers in Rome to *pray for him*. The brethren in Rome believed in the same *Lord Jesus Christ,* and they were indwelt by the same *love of the Spirit.* Even though they had never met one another, Paul knew that their prayers on his behalf would be answered. The interesting word for *"strive together with me"* is *"sunagonizomai,"* which means *"to agonize or struggle."* Paul, having being saved out of Judaism, knew exactly what he was facing in Jerusalem. He wanted the Jew and Gentile believers in Christ to *fight* with him in prayer. Several reasons why Paul needed their prayers:

- ***That he might be delivered from the unbelievers in Judaea***
- ***That the Jewish saints in Jerusalem would accept his offering from the Gentile saints***
- ***That he might come to Rome with joy***
- ***That it might be God's will***
- ***That he might be ★ refreshed with the believers in Rome***

"Now the God of peace be with you all. Amen" - Paul ends with his own prayer for the believers in Rome. After all of the instructions that Paul has given to them, he is praying that there will be no disorder in their community, and that the *God of peace* would be with them.

★ *(Paul would eventually come to Rome, but he would be in chains. He was under house arrest for two years in Rome.* **Acts 28:30.** *Yet, he had the opportunity to share the gospel of Christ with the Jews in the synagogue of Rome and to many Gentile prisoners. It is believed that after being released, Paul traveled to Spain and came back to Rome in shackles. He died a martyr's death in 67 AD.)*

CHAPTER SIXTEEN

Paul Commends Phoibe

> **Romans 16:1-2** - ***I commend unto you Phebe our sister, which is a servant of the church which is at Cenchrea: That ye receive her in the Lord, as becometh saints, and that ye assist her in whatsoever business she hath need of you: for she hath been a succourer of many, and of myself also.***

The first person that Paul names in this long list of individuals is *Phebe*, or the Greek, *Phoibe*, pronounced *"Foy-bay."* Many of the early Christians in the Roman world had pagan names, so there is no need to change their names.

This passage has caused a lot of debate and division over the centuries. Was *Phoibe* a *deaconess*? Should there be deaconesses in the local church? The word for *"servant"* here is *"diakonos"* and means *"a waiter, servant, minister,"* and it is where the word *"deacon"* comes from. This is the only time that Paul refers to a *woman* in this light. It also shows that Paul did not think that ⋆ women were less spiritual than men. No matter what some church opinions may say, *Phoibe* was a ⋆⋆ *deaconess* in the church at *Cenchrea*, which was a port city of Corinth. Evidently this was not a big issue in Bible times as it is today. Paul thought enough of *Phoibe's* service that he called her *"sister," a "servant,"* and *"saint."*

★ *(Jesus Christ included women within His inner circle of friends. While they were not part of the 12 men disciples, they were considered women disciples, or the Hebrew "talmidot." They provided finances for His ministry, and followed Him all the way to Jerusalem from Galilee.* **Luke 8:1-3***)*

★★ *(This does not mean that Phoibe was an ordained or clerical deaconess as many churches recognize today, but she was a true servant of the Lord. The design was for the women to attend to the needs of other women and to the children.* **(Titus 2:3-5)** *There is not enough evidence in the New Testament to clearly determine that there was an official capacity for a deaconess, but it does not disqualify her either. If a local church decides to have deaconesses, it needs to follow the biblical understanding and not the modern-day perspective. Again, a deaconess would not be ordained officially, but she would help women when they were water baptized. She could also serve the sick, the poor, the strangers, and the needy. Deacons and deaconesses are not to think that they are people of authority, but people who serve others.)*

"That ye receive her in the Lord, as becometh saints, and that ye assist her in whatsoever business she hath need of you: for she hath been a succourer of many, and of myself also" **–** Apparently *Phoibe* was entrusted with carrying the letter from Corinth to Rome, and Paul sends an advance recommendation of this *sister* in Christ. Paul wanted the Roman believers to receive *Phoibe* and support her during her stay there. *Phoibe* had proven herself worthy as a *succourer,* or the Greek *prostatis, of many,* including Paul himself. *Phoibe* had been a *patron and a* *protectress* for others, and Paul wanted the Roman Christians to protect and provide for her.

> **Romans 16:3-5a** - ***Greet Priscilla and Aquila my helpers in Christ Jesus: Who have for my life laid down their own necks: unto whom not only I give thanks, but also all the churches of the Gentiles. Likewise greet the church that is in their house.***

Never having traveled to Rome, Paul was familiar with numerous people there. The missionary couple, *Priscilla and Aquila,* were ⋆ from Rome and were tentmakers, as was Paul. They are mentioned together six times in the New Testament. **(Acts 18:2-3, 18, 26, Romans 16:3, I Cor. 16:19, 2 Tim. 4:19)** *Priscilla* was the more prominent of the two; therefore, she is listed first in all but one. Paul may have very well received the knowledge of the house churches in Rome from them. *They not only were helpers in Christ Jesus, but they laid down their lives for Paul.*

⋆ *(According to* **Acts 18:1-2**, *Priscilla and Aquila had been expelled from Rome by the Emperor Claudius in 49 AD. This is the only place where Aquila is listed first.)*

"Likewise greet the church that is in their house" - It is believed that there were at least 15 house or tenement churches in Rome with each one having small groups. The believers knew that the ⋆ glory of God dwelt inside of them, not in fancy-adorned buildings. There were no church buildings until the form of the Catholic Church in the early 4th century. *Priscilla and Aquila* may have had one of the largest house churches, and they were teachers of the Sacred Scriptures. They are the ones who explained the way of God more accurately to *Apollos* in **Acts 18:26.**

★ *(God's glory came to dwell in the Temple built by Solomon after his fervent and humble prayer* **(2 Chronicles 6-7).** *God chose to allow His presence again evident through the radiance and splendor of His glory to remain in the Temple for centuries. Yet after the Jews had proven their determination to continue in false, idolatrous worship, the presence of God's glory did eventually leave the Jerusalem Temple prior to its looting and destruction by the Babylonians.* **(Ezekiel 11:23)** *Even when the second Temple was rebuilt in its place after the return from Jewish exile, God's glory did not occupy it. Moreover, there is no record of the shimmering, luminous glory ever again occupying an earthly building. God's glory was not in the Temple in Jerusalem during Jesus' earthly ministry. The shepherds saw the glory appear in the sky as angels announced the birth of the Savior* **(Luke 2:9).** *Indeed, the coming of Christ in the flesh was, in essence, God coming to dwell with human beings* **(John 1:1, 14; Matthew 1:23).** *After His death and resurrection, He would live within the believers through the Holy Spirit.* **(Colossians 1:27, 2 Cor. 6:16)** *The first century followers of Christ knew that God did not dwell in buildings, and they would never have imagined the emphasis being placed on church buildings that would come later.)*

> ***Salute the brethren which are in Laodicea, and Nymphas, and the church which is in his house.*** **Colossians 4:15**
>
> ***And to our beloved Apphia, and Archippus our fellowsoldier, and to the church in thy house:*** **Philemon 2**
>
> **Romans 16:5b-9 -** ***Salute my well-beloved Epaenetus, who is the firstfruits of Achaia unto Christ. Greet Mary, who bestowed much labour***

on us. Salute Andronicus and Junia, my kinsmen, and my fellow-prisoners, who are of note among the apostles, who also were in Christ before me. Greet Amplias my beloved in the Lord. Salute Urbane, our helper in Christ, and Stachys my beloved.

Paul is mentioning people that he knew from within the house churches. All that is known about many of these individuals is what is mentioned here. Having one's name listed in the Holy Bible shows how important he was in the cause of Christ in the first century. *Epaenetus* was among the very first converts of *Achaia*, where Corinth was located. His name implies that he was probably a Gentile. Paul did not use the word *beloved*, or the Greek *agapetos*, very cheaply. This Greek word is used many times in the gospels when referring to Jesus being the *"beloved."*

Mary, comes from the Hebrew ***Miriam,*** and suggests that she was a Jewish believer. Paul further mentioned that she had worked hard for the church in Rome.

Andronicus and Junia, husband and wife, were believed to be Jewish believers from Jerusalem. Three important points about this Jewish couple:

- ***They were fellow prisoners with Paul***
- ***They had a high reputation among the Apostles***
- ***They came to believe in Christ before Paul***

Amplias, a Roman name, was divinely *loved* by Paul. There is a tomb dating from the last of the first century in the earliest Christian catacomb of Rome that bears the name AMPLIAS.

Urbane is the Greek form of the Latin, ***Urbanus.*** Paul lists his name as being *our helper in Christ.* Paul is not listing names of great theologians, but common people who became not only followers of Jesus, but who contributed much to the cause of God's kingdom.

Stachys my beloved must have been close to Paul. There are two strong traditions that Stachys may have been one of the 70 disciples mentioned in Luke 10:1, and the second Bishop of Byzantium from 38-54 AD.

> **Romans 16:10-12 - *Salute Apelles approved in Christ. Salute them which are of ⋆ Aristobulus' household. Salute Herodion my kinsman. Greet them that be of the household of ⋆ Narcissus, which are in the Lord. Salute Tryphena and Tryphosa, who labour in the Lord. Salute the beloved Persis, which laboured much in the Lord.***

Apelles had been tested, tried, and proved to be a respected believer in Christ. We can have the assurance that we are presently *approved* in Christ. It is interesting that we find two possible men, *Aristobulus* and *Herodian*, who were included in the family of king Herod. **(Matt. 2:1)** Notice that Paul salutes, *"them which are of the household of Aristobulus,"* but not *Aristobulus* himself.

⋆ *(It is not known if Aristobulus was alive or deceased at the time of Paul's writing. There is a strong tradition that Aristobulus was ordained a Bishop by Barnabas or Paul. He later went to Britain and converted many souls to Christ. Paul also greets the household of Narcissus, who is believed to have been one of the 70 disciples.* **(Luke 10:1)** *He was ordained as the Bishop of Athens.)*

Tryphena and Tryphosa **-** These two women were sisters, and they have interesting names. Their Greek names mean *"luxuriousness and voluptuous."* This may describe the lifestyles of these women before they were born again. Whatever the case may be, they were now *laboring in the Lord* and serving the church in Rome. As Paul varies his style in his brief comments about various people, he commends *Persis*, a Persian name, who was another woman believer in Rome who had *labored much in the Lord.* Paul commends her with special affection.

> **Romans 16:13-15 - *Salute Rufus chosen in the Lord, and his mother and mine. Salute Asyncritus, Phlegon, Hermas, Patrobas, Hermes, and the brethren which are with them. Salute Philologus, and Julia, Nereus, and his sister, and Olympas, and all the saints which are with them.***

It is very likely that the *Rufus* mentioned here as being chosen in the Lord is the same *Rufus* who is mentioned in **Mark 15:21:**

> ***And they compel one Simon a Cyrenian, who passed by, coming out of the country, the father of Alexander and Rufus, to bear his cross.***

Mark's gospel was written particularly to the Christians living in Rome. The story of *Simon the Cyrene,* the father of *Rufus*, would have been well known in the churches in Rome. Notice that Paul mentioned the *mother of Rufus* as well. If this is true, what a powerful thought to be one of the children of the man who carried the cross for Jesus!

"Salute Asyncritus, Phlegon, Hermas, Patrobas, Hermes, and the brethren which are with them. Salute Philologus, and Julia, Nereus, and his sister, and Olympas, and all the saints

which are with them." **-** Little is known about these individuals other than some of their names were found inscribed as members of Caesar's household, such as *Patrobas* and *Nereus.* Notice that Paul calls them *"brethren"* and *"saints."* We are reminded here that only heaven will reveal how many people were believers in Christ from Caesar's household:

> ***All the saints salute you, chiefly they that are of Caesar's household.*** **Philippians 4:22**

> **Romans 16:16 -** ***Salute one another with an holy kiss. The churches of Christ salute you.***

One of the ancient Middle Eastern customs was a ⋆ *holy kiss,* a sign of their joyful fellowship. This custom is found in five other places in the New Testament: **(Matt. 26:49, I Cor. 16:20, 2 Cor. 13:12, I Thess. 5:26, and I Peter 5:14)**

⋆ *(Many people believe that this was only cultural and does not have to be obeyed today. People in our culture may feel uncomfortable with the idea of a holy kiss. However, it is unwise to totally dismiss such passages as being cultural. One should not feel ashamed or embarrassed to show this affection to a fellow believer. It is based on personal preference.)*

"The churches of Christ salute you." **-** All of the churches of Jesus Christ throughout the Roman world salute these people who have been mentioned. What an honor! All of the churches that belong to Christ are bound together and serve the same Lord! This unity has been broken down for centuries, and we can see why our world is in chaos; the churches are not serving Christ in unity.

Paul Issues a Warning

> **Romans 16:17-18 - *Now I beseech you, brethren, mark them which cause divisions and offences contrary to the doctrine which ye have learned; and avoid them. For they that are such serve not our Lord Jesus Christ, but their own belly; and by good words and fair speeches deceive the hearts of the simple.***

Paul now tells the believers in Rome to avoid the ones who *cause divisions that cause pointless factions.* If someone goes against what Paul has taught, he is to be *marked out.* The false teachers who came into the churches with *smooth speeches and flattery* were trying to make merchandise out of them so they could *eat well.* Their ways are sly and subtle, and they *deceive the hearts of the simple.* The church must protect the sheep from these wolves in sheep's clothing *who are not servants of our Lord Jesus Christ.* If false teachers were a problem in the first century, how much more are they are problem today? The Apostle Peter spoke about the false prophets that would be among the people:

> ***But there were false prophets also among the people, even as there shall be false teachers among you, who privily shall bring in damnable heresies, even denying the Lord that bought them, and bring upon themselves swift destruction. And many shall follow their pernicious ways; by reason of whom the way of truth shall be evil spoken of. And through covetousness shall they with feigned words make merchandise of you: whose judgment now of a long time lingereth not, and their damnation slumbereth not.* 2 Peter 2:1-3**

> **Romans 16:19-20 -** ***For your obedience is come abroad unto all men. I am glad therefore on your behalf: but yet I would have you wise unto that which is good, and simple concerning evil. And the God of peace shall bruise Satan under your feet shortly. The grace of our Lord Jesus Christ be with you. Amen.***

The *obedience* of the church in Rome had been reported everywhere across land and sea. Yet they must remain diligent against the attacks of those who would try to divide them. Paul is telling them to spend more time focusing on the *good more than the evil things.* The Greek word here for "simple" is *"akeraios,"* and it means *"unmixed, pure."* The believers in Rome are being warned about mixing the *good with the evil.* This is one of Satan's undermined schemes, to mix the truth with the false so that the immature believers cannot know the difference.

"And the God of peace shall bruise Satan under your feet shortly. The grace of our Lord Jesus Christ be with you. Amen." **-** This verse contains a reference to **Genesis 3:15:**

> ***And I will put enmity between thee and the woman, and between thy seed and her seed; it shall bruise thy head, and thou shalt bruise his heel.***

If the believers in Rome are faithful to do what Paul has told them, *the God of peace shall bruise Satan under their feet.* When Paul mentions that this will place *shortly,* or the Greek, *tachos,* does not mean that God will bruise Satan *soon,* but focuses on the swiftness with which the action will be accomplished. The *bruising* is not only a present reality, but it is also viewed as something in the future when Jesus will crush Satan on behalf of all humanity in **Revelation 20:1-10.**

"The grace of our Lord Jesus Christ be with you. Amen." **-** Paul's heart is so filled with love for the believers in Rome that he gives them three benedictions. The first one was in **Romans 15:33** and the last one is in **Romans 16:24.** The little word with is *"meta,"* and means *"among you."* What sweet fellowship there is when the grace of our Lord Jesus Christ is among His people!

Personal Greetings

> **Romans 16:21-23 - *Timotheus my workfellow, and Lucius, and Jason, and Sosipater, my kinsmen, salute you. I Tertius, who wrote this epistle, salute you in the Lord. Gaius mine host, and of the whole church, saluteth you. Erastus the chamberlain of the city saluteth you, and Quartus a brother.***

Paul now remembers to pass on some personal greetings from four of the special believers. *Timotheus*, or ★ *Timothy*, was a close and trusted associate of Paul.

★ *(Timothy was the first Bishop of the church at Ephesus and was the recipient of the letters* **1 Timothy** *and* **2 Timothy.** *History records that at the age of 80, Timothy tried to stop a procession honoring the goddess Diana in Ephesus. He started preaching the gospel and was dragged through the streets and beaten. The year was 97AD.)*

Lucius was a prophet and teacher from Cyrene. **(Acts 13:1)** Jason is mentioned four times in **Acts 17:5-9,** who fell victim to a mob assault in Thessalonica. *Sosipater* is also called *Sopater* in

Acts 20:4. History records that *Sosipater* and *Jason* won many people to Christ on the Greek island of Corfu and died at an old age. These men were fellow Jewish believers with Paul who sent their personal greetings to the church in Rome.

Tertius was Paul's secretary, or *amanuensis*. Paul dictated the letter to the Romans while *Tertius* wrote it down. *Tertius* realized that he had been used by the Lord to copy down part of the Holy Scriptures. He became a Bishop in Iconium, a city in Central Asia Minor, present-day Turkey. He was martyred there.

Gaius was baptized by Paul, **(I Cor. 1:14)** and he served as Paul's host in Corinth. He may also be the same Gaius that is mentioned in **3 John 1.** ⋆ *Erastus*, the treasurer of Corinth, is also mentioned in **2 Timothy 4:20.** The last man who sends a greeting is *Quartus a brother.* It is recorded that *Quartus* suffered martyrdom in Athens and was tortured by casting him into the fire.

⋆ *(In 1929 an inscription mentioning an Erastus was found near a paved area northeast of the theater of Corinth. It has been dated to the mid-first century and reads, "Erastus in return for his aedileship paved it at his own expense.")*

Doxology

> **Romans 16:24-27 - *The grace of our Lord Jesus Christ be with you all. Amen. Now to him that is of power to stablish you according to my gospel, and the preaching of Jesus Christ, according to the revelation of the mystery, which was kept secret since the world began, But now is made manifest, and by the scriptures of the prophets, according to the commandment of the everlasting God, made known***

to all nations for the obedience of faith: To God only wise, be glory through Jesus Christ for ever. Amen.

The emphasis here is the *establishment of the believers in the faith.* Only God has the power to accomplish this *by means of the gospel. The preaching of Jesus Christ was according to the revelation of the mystery, which was kept secret since the world began.* The Eternal God's *mystery* had been designed and then revealed to Paul how the Church would consist of Jews and Gentiles together who trusted in the finished work of Christ. This *revelation* was not given to the Prophets of the Old Testament, but to the Apostles in the New Testament. The Apostle Paul had been given the revelation about the blindness of Israel until the fullness of the Gentiles be brought in. **(Romans 11:25)** The main content of this *revelation* was that salvation would be preached to the Gentiles. All of this was according to the commandment of the everlasting God. The ones who received this revelation were all the *nations*, meaning the Gentiles *who were obedient to the faith.* Knowing this mystery would help the church in Rome be established in the faith. In summary, let us review three ways that God will establish the believers in Rome:

* ***Through the mystery that had been kept secret since the world began***
* ***Through the mystery being revealed to the Apostle Paul***
* ***Through the preaching of Jesus Christ***

"To God only wise, be glory through Jesus Christ for ever. Amen." - The *wisdom of Almighty God* is beyond man's comprehension. What Paul was preaching was not his or any other man's invention. It is only fitting for Paul to close this epistle by giving all of the *glory to God* through the work that He had accomplished *through Jesus Christ.* Not only did God glorify Himself once through the work of Jesus Christ, He will glorify Himself *forever and ever.* It is also very fitting that the Jewish Paul closes this letter with the Hebrew *"Amane,"* or "so let it be!"

A NOTE FROM THE EDITORS

The book of Romans is the New Testament's longest, most structured, and most detailed description of Christian theology. Carroll has tackled this book by laying out the core of Paul's gospel message: salvation by grace alone through faith alone.

Carroll has explained what Paul wrote about the good news of Jesus Christ in accurate and clear terms. He has addressed the conflicts between law and grace, between Jews and Gentiles, and between sin and righteousness.

Carroll also has given clear practical applications to Paul's messages. He has defined the meanings of the original languages, both Hebrew and Greek, in order to help the reader have a more thorough and complete understanding of Paul's passages.

Thank you, Carroll, for always teaching about Jesus Christ through your books, sermons, and your music.

It is our prayer that anyone who reads Carroll's book will come away with a deeper understanding of what Paul wrote about in the book of Romans and have a closer relationship to Jesus Christ.

Editors,

Virginia and Glenn Duggin

www.ingramcontent.com/pod-product-compliance
Lightning Source LLC
LaVergne TN
LVHW020540100826
845148LV00010B/1552

* 9 7 8 1 6 1 3 1 4 9 4 4 7 *